BE
THOU
MY
THE POWER OF CHRISTIAN MUSIC™
VISION

Published by Standard Publishing, Cincinnati, Ohio. A division of Standex International Corporation. Printed in the United States of America.

Cover and interior design by Rule29.

ISBN 0-7847-1543-2

11 10 09 08 07 06 05   9 8 7 6 5 4 3 2 1

BE
THOU
MY
THE POWER OF CHRISTIAN MUSIC™
VISION

DEVOTIONS FROM
THE LYRICS OF
POPULAR MUSIC

// COMPILED BY LINDSAY BLACK //

Standard
PUBLISHING
Bringing The Word to Life™

Cincinnati, Ohio

/// TABLE OF CONTENTS ///

INTRODUCTION

It's rather awe inspiring that the God who created *EVERYTHING* uses the entire universe to speak to us, isn't it? God created the earth for his glory, and he uses his creation to reveal himself to us in ways that can help us actually begin to know him more intimately.

When you take a moment to consider it, the best Christian music lyrics are those that help us deepen our relationships with God. These lyrics convey a truth that an artist has discovered for himself about God or an experience that an artist had that drew him closer to God. There is much to be gained by letting God use Christian lyrics to speak to us just as he does through the rest of creation.

Be Thou My Vision encompasses the lyrics of more than fifty songs and the reactions of real people—from ministers and artists to a corn geneticist and a rocket scientist—who have connected with God and music in a way that is unique to them. The diversity among the contributing writers poignantly illustrates the fact that music speaks to people—a wide variety of people—and it affects each of us differently.

The devotions relate to us the impact these particular song lyrics have had on each particular author. As you meditate on these devotions, don't limit yourself to the experience and expression of one author; let God speak directly to *you* through the lyrics. The prayer directives and "cues" following each devotion are intended to challenge you to dig deeper, take an honest look at yourself, and apply what you've discovered to your life.

Hopefully *Be Thou My Vision* will challenge you to reflect on these lyrics for yourself, innovate your devotional time, and enhance your personal worship. And just maybe it will help you see with new eyes the universe that God has created and listen more closely to the things that he's trying to say to you through his creation.

GIVE US CLEAN HANDS

// PERFORMED BY CHARLIE HALL //

We bow our hearts, we bend our knees
O Spirit, come make us humble
We turn our eyes from evil things
O Lord, we cast down our idols

So give us clean hands, give us pure hearts
Let us not lift our souls to another
And give us clean hands, give us pure hearts
Let us not lift our souls to another

O God, let us be a generation that seeks,
That seeks Your face, O God of Jacob
O God, let us be a generation that seeks,
That seeks Your face, O God of Jacob

/// GOD OF JACOB ///

AMANDA BOWER

God didn't do much of the obviously spectacular through Jacob. He didn't give Jacob power to part the Red Sea, or heal a disabled person, or prophesy to a nation. Called "the grasper" because he was born clutching the heel of his brother Esau, Jacob managed to steal a birthright by bartering stew, lie and cheat to gain his father's blessing, and then run like a coward to a faraway land.

So why did God choose to make Jacob the father of twelve sons who would later be the heads of the twelve tribes of Israel?

In Genesis 28:15 the Lord spoke to Jacob in a dream, promising to watch over him and never leave him. From that point forward, Jacob reasoned that if God would take care of him, then Jacob would call him Lord of his life. So we see here in the life of Jacob God's willingness and power to forgive. Exodus 33:19 says that God will have mercy and compassion on those whom he chooses. And Romans 9:16 tells us that forgiveness does not depend on man's desire or effort, but on God's mercy. So what does this mean for us?

The answer can be found in Exodus 9:16, where God says, "I have raised you up for this very purpose, that I might show you my power and that my name might be proclaimed in all the earth" *(NIV)*. Just as Jacob responded to God's promise to protect him by submitting to his mercy, we also are called to cast down our idols, to turn from our sin, and to ask that we be made clean in order to be used for God's purposes. God's perfect plan offers salvation to imperfect people. Through Jacob we see that we are never too bad to be forgiven and that our history does not inhibit God from carrying out his will.

The God who forgave and blessed Jacob is the same God who offers to forgive and bless anyone who seeks his face. God continues to use his power to cleanse the hands and purify the hearts of all who humbly bow and surrender to be used as instruments in his merciful hand.

/// YOUR CUE ///

When have you asked to be made humble? When should you have asked?

_____

_____

_____

_____

_____

_____

_____

_____

_____

_____

What idols do you need to cast down so that you can be used by God?

_____

_____

_____

_____

_____

Have you ever had an Exodus 9:16 moment in which it has been obvious that God has been working and showing his power through you? What did that feel like?

_____

_____

_____

_____

_____

_____

_____

_____

_____

_____

_____

_____

_____

_____

_____

IT IS WELL
WITH MY SOUL

// PERFORMED BY JENNIFER KNAPP //

When peace, like a river, attendeth my way,
when sorrows like sea billows roll;
whatever my lot, thou hast taught me to say,
It is well, it is well with my soul.

It is well with my soul,
It is well, it is well with my soul.

Though Satan should buffet, though trials should come,
let this blest assurance control,
that Christ has regarded my helpless estate,
and hath shed his own blood for my soul.

My sin, oh, the bliss of this glorious thought!
My sin, not in part but the whole,
is nailed to the cross, and I bear it no more,
praise the Lord, praise the Lord, O my soul!

And, Lord, haste the day when my faith shall be sight,
the clouds be rolled back as a scroll;
the trump shall resound, and the Lord shall descend,
even so, it is well with my soul.

/// WHY ME? ///

AMANDA BOWER

It is sometimes difficult to be truly content with what we have. It's hard to swim against that ever-raging current of want. Instead of asking, "Lord, why am I allowing the peace and contentedness that you have given me to be stolen?" we ask, "Why me?" when life isn't going the way we had hoped.

But God's will for us does not change according to passing circumstances. As presented in 1 Thessalonians 5:16-18, God's will is sovereign. "Be joyful always; pray continually; give thanks in all circumstances, for this is God's will for you in Christ Jesus" *(NIV).* I came to realize that I often fail to fully embrace what God desires for me. Instead I allow discontent to sap my joy and overshadow all I have to be thankful for.

I am beginning to see how God demonstrates his power to give contentment to those who choose to follow his will. Just recently a friend of mine showed me the essence of what it means to truly thank God in all circumstances. Amidst a legitimate reason to sit and wallow in pity, she prayed a prayer of thanks for the good things that had happened in her life, pushing the bad aside for a while. I am learning to be content with what I have and to give thanks for the good things *and* the bad.

I am encouraged by what Horatio Spafford writes in "It Is Well with My Soul": "Whatever my lot, thou has taught me to say, 'It is well, it is well with my soul.'" So when Satan attacks and attempts to steal my joy and peace, still I can be thankful that I have the assurance of Heaven through Christ's sacrifice for me. I can be thankful that I no longer bear the burden of sin—that it was nailed to the cross with Jesus. I can give thanks that even if the Lord does not return today, he is in fact returning to take me home someday. And all of that gives me a reason to be joyful always! God provides everything we need in order to find contentment in such a discontent world.

Pray a prayer of thanksgiving to God for the wealth of things for which you can be thankful. Thank him that he is ever-present no matter what goes awry in your life.

/// YOUR CUE ///

What is one part of 1 Thessalonians 5:16-18 that you could begin to work on this week?

_____

_____

_____

_____

_____

_____

Who do you allow to steal your joy?

_____

_____

_____

_____

_____

_____

Have you ever made a list of all the things you have to be thankful for? Take time to do that now and remember these in times of discontent.

_____
_____
_____
_____
_____
_____
_____
_____
_____
_____
_____

MORE TO LIFE

// PERFORMED BY STACIE ORRICO //

I've got it all, but I feel so deprived
I go up, I come down and I'm emptier inside
Tell me what is this thing that I feel like I'm missing
And why can't I let it go

There's gotta be more to life . . .
Than chasing down every temporary high to satisfy me
Cause the more that I'm . . .
Trippin' out thinkin' there must be more to life
Well it's life, but I'm sure . . . There's gotta be more
(Than wanting more)

I've got the time and I'm wasting it slowly
Here in this moment I'm halfway out the door
Onto the next thing, I'm searching for something that's missing

I'm wanting more
I'm always waiting on something other than this
Why am I feelin' like there's something I missed . . .
Always . . . Always . . .

More to life
There's gotta be more to life (more to life)
There's gotta be more to life (more)
More to my life

/// *SOMETHING'S MISSING* ///

AMANDA BOWER

I t makes no matter who you are or where you live—odds are that there has been a time when you've wondered if there really is anything more to life. Something is missing. Clothes and music and relationships and activities only get you so far because, fundamentally, there's no continuity, no driving force or foundation, no ultimate purpose found in them.

Our temporary highs come in a myriad of shapes and sizes, but no matter what you consider yours to be, the fact is that we as human beings tend to travel from thing to thing in search of our ultimate high. When our security is based on day-to-day doings and feelings, the real power—that foundation and force upon which a healthy life should be based—is missing.

When we step back from the daily distractions and see them for what they truly are, the things of this world no longer satisfy and we feel alone and empty. In the same way, when we take time to examine the risk and the result of the rituals we become accustomed to—and they no longer yield the feeling of purpose that they did the day before— then what more is there? Is there really anything more to my life, or is this it?

All too often we experience serious consequences before we fully realize the futility of trying to fill up our lives with the stuff of this world. By the time reality hits, relationships have been damaged, and not only are we experiencing serious disillusionment with the world, we're also doubting and questioning God—angry that we have not yet found our reason to live. The fact is, we will never find our purpose if we allow the things of the world to take our focus off God.

Pretty grim. But things need not stay that way. God has the power to provide purpose in this world of wanderers. When we finally discover our life's purpose in Christ and accept the glorious plans he has for us, we'll discover that the missing piece has been within reach all along. "It's in Christ that we find out who we are and what we are living for. Long before we first heard of Christ . . . he had his eye on us, had designs on us for glorious living, part of the overall purpose he is working out in everything and everyone" (Ephesians 1:11, 12, *Message*).

PRAYER FOCUS

Pray that God will begin revealing bits and pieces of his plan to you today. Revel in the truth that there is "more to life" and that you know where to find it.

/// YOUR CUE ///

What are the temporary highs that you rely on during your day-to-day journey? In what ways are these beneficial? destructive? futile?

_____

_____

_____

_____

_____

_____

_____

_____

_____

Have you ever looked forward to and idealized an event, stage of life, or a person—and been let down?

_____

_____

_____

_____

_____

_____

_____

_____

_____

_____

_____

How did the focus on the temporary high make you feel afterward? If that was discouraging, then how could a firm foundation of purpose, rooted in the love of God and his control over your life, produce a different reaction?

_____

_____

_____

_____

_____

_____

_____

_____

_____

_____

UNTITLED HYMN (COME TO JESUS)

// PERFORMED BY CHRIS RICE //

Weak and wounded sinner
Lost and left to die
Oh, raise your head, for love is passing
  by
Come to Jesus
Come to Jesus
Come to Jesus and live!

Now your burden's lifted
And carried far away
And precious blood has washed away the
  stain, so
Sing to Jesus
Sing to Jesus
Sing to Jesus and live!

And like a newborn baby
Don't be afraid to crawl
And remember when you walk
Sometimes we fall . . . so
Fall on Jesus
Fall on Jesus
Fall on Jesus and live!

Sometimes the way is lonely
And steep and filled with pain
So if your sky is dark and pours the rain,
  then
Cry to Jesus
Cry to Jesus
Cry to Jesus and live!

Oh, and when the love spills over
And music fills the night
And when you can't contain your joy
  inside, then
Dance for Jesus
Dance for Jesus
Dance for Jesus and live!

And with your final heartbeat
Kiss the world good-bye
Then go in peace, and laugh on glory's
  side, and
Fly to Jesus
Fly to Jesus
Fly to Jesus and live!

/// LOVE IS PASSING BY ///

AMANDA BOWER

m I the only one who is struggling with this sin? No one else could possibly understand. No one is tempted the way that I am. How could anyone love and forgive someone like me? It is with these words of loneliness, grief, and weakness that I so often fall at the feet of the Lord.

Wading in pools of failure, the clouds never part and the rains never cease. Fear of failure keeps us complacent, and our inability to erase sin keeps us cowering and ashamed even when love passes by. In "Untitled Hymn" Chris Rice calls the sinner to come to Jesus—he who feels unworthy to be loved and undeserving of forgiveness is considered worthy and deserving through the sacrifice of Christ.

This is a vivid echo of Christ's loving call to all of us: "Come to me, all you who are weary and burdened, and I will give you rest" (Matthew 11:28, *NIV*). After we accept this invitation, there is inevitable joy; we praise God daily for his peace. Our newfound confidence and freedom are refreshing. We even share that joy with other people.

And then we fall down again. And again. And again. And we feel even more worthless than the last time. Repeated sin becomes a wall that can keep us from closeness with God. Not because we are so filthy and unworthy that he doesn't want us, but because we begin to believe the lie that God's love is conditional.

When we exile our sinful selves and shamefully wallow in the loneliness and self-pity that result, we miss the abundant life that God promises to all. Though we can never balance a scale of good works and sin, God's grace covers over the sin of yesterday, today, and tomorrow. Through all stages of the predictably sinful life, God's powerful forgiveness and loving-kindness are unchanging. And they are ours for the taking if we would just raise our heads to see that his love is passing before us. If we come to Jesus, he will make us new and give us life again.

You aren't the only one who struggles with sin. We all do and will continue to—but God will never refuse our remorse or resist when we repent. So "come to Jesus and live!"

PRAYER FOCUS

Pray to God for forgiveness, being confident in the knowledge that he receives you again and again no matter what and will always be there when you call.

/// YOUR CUE ///

Jesus is always by your side. Do you ever forget that you have someone else cheering on your team? What could help you remember?

_____

_____

_____

_____

_____

_____

_____

_____

Does a fear of failure and of submitting to a higher power keep you from coming to Jesus and accepting his loving-kindness and forgiveness?

_____

_____

_____

_____

_____

_____

_____

_____

_____

_____

GREAT LIGHT OF THE WORLD

// **PERFORMED BY BEBO NORMAN** //

Sometimes at night
I am afraid
I cover my eyes,
Cover my shame
So here in the dark
Broken apart
Come with your light
And fill up my heart

O great light of the world,
Fill up my soul
I'm half a man here
So come make me whole
O great light of the world,
Come to impart
The light of your grace
To fill up my heart

The wind of this world
Can push us around
Folding us up
Backing us down
But here in the dark
I'm not alone
So come with your strength
And carry me home

O great light of the world,
Fill up my soul
I'm half a man here
So come make me whole
O great light of the world,
Come to impart
The light of your grace
To fill up my heart
The light of your grace
To fill up my heart

/// DISPELLING DARKNESS ///

AMY LEE

envision a sunny afternoon in the forest. Picture all the trees with their low-hanging branches and their exposed roots jutting up here and there along a winding path. You see the squirrels and other creatures scurrying about, and you hear the wind gently rustling the trees. How peaceful this scene is.

Now, envision the same place but in the darkest hour of the night. The once peaceful rustling trees send a shiver down your spine. You trip over the roots and get snagged by the branches. The activity of the animals startles you, and you keep looking over your shoulder, straining to see what may be lurking in the dark. Fear invades the peace; the place that once was so serene now becomes the stuff of nightmares.

But in reality the place itself hasn't changed. The trees do not lean down any further, the roots are no higher, the animals are not readying themselves for an attack, and the wind is not taunting you. It is merely our perspective that has changed. It is the darkness, not our circumstances, that intimidates us.

Now transfer this idea to our own lives. There are areas of our lives that are similar to the forest in the dead of night—those things that haunt us and continually trip us up. They cover us with shame and guilt and leave us with a sense of hopelessness. We need to turn these things over to Jesus who said, "I am the light of the world. Whoever follows me will never walk in darkness, but will have the light of life" (John 8:12, *NIV*). When light comes in, darkness has to flee.

Often, Jesus uses other Christians to help us remain in his light. James urges: "Therefore confess your sins to each other and pray for each other so that you may be healed" (James 5:16, *NIV*). Jesus longs to shine on all of our haunted places to uncover the truth. He desires to set us free and make us whole. He has promised to do just that, and he is always faithful.

/// YOUR CUE ///

Is there any area of your life where darkness has been allowed to remain? Right now will you ask Jesus, the light of the world, to shine on that area of your life?

_____

_____

_____

_____

_____

_____

_____

_____

_____

If you are dealing with a very resistant problem, is there a trusted Christian friend or counselor you could discuss it with?

_____

_____

_____

_____

_____

_____

_____

_____

_____

_____

I CAN ONLY IMAGINE

// PERFORMED BY MERCY ME //

I can only imagine
What it will be like
When I walk
By your side
I can only imagine
What my eyes will see
When your face
Is before me
I can only imagine

Surrounded by your glory,
what will my heart feel
Will I dance for you, Jesus,
or in awe of you be still
Will I stand in your presence
or to my knees will I fall
Will I sing hallelujah
will I be able to speak at all
I can only imagine

I can only imagine
When that day comes
And I find myself
Standing in the Son
I can only imagine
When all I will do
Is forever
Forever worship you
I can only imagine

Words by Bart Millard. © 1999 Simpleville
Music (ASCAP). All rights reserved. Used
by permission.

/// MISCONCEPTIONS ///

AMY LEE

as a child I had many misconceptions of Heaven. The cartoon/comic strip view of Heaven being a place where everyone sits around on clouds strumming their harps all day was probably the most influential. The daughter of a preacher, I was in Sunday school every single Sunday. While I'm sure that my teachers painted a more accurate view of Heaven, for some reason my young mind fixed on the former rather than the latter. As I grew up, my views of Heaven and God gradually changed. In high school I began to be more excited about Heaven. But that was balanced by my dreams of going to college, being married, having kids, and growing old—dreams that prompted me to tell God, "I'm not ready yet."

I used to contemplate Heaven with tempered enthusiasm. Then the first time that I heard "I Can Only Imagine," I began to cry as I really thought, *What will I do when I stand in the presence of God?* That was a turning point in my life—the first time I thought about Heaven in that light.

As my intimacy with God deepens, my anticipation of Heaven is heightened. God is revealing to me that Heaven will be wonderful because of the one who is there. And in Matthew Jesus describes Heaven: "The Kingdom of Heaven is like a treasure that a man discovered hidden in a field. In his excitement, he hid it again and sold everything he owned to get enough money to buy the field—and to get the treasure, too!" (Matthew 13:44).

My longing to be in Heaven grows daily. I am finally getting to the point where I can honestly say that I can't wait to go to Heaven. I desire that this thought come into play in every decision that I make—that I would be ever mindful of the fact that this world is not my home.

/// YOUR CUE ///

What do you envision when you think about Heaven?

_____
_____
_____
_____
_____
_____
_____
_____
_____
_____

Are your perceptions based on the truth according to God's Word?

_____
_____
_____
_____
_____
_____
_____

What do you anticipate your reaction will be when you see Jesus?

_____
_____
_____
_____
_____
_____
_____
_____
_____
_____
_____

IT'S ALRIGHT

// PERFORMED BY THIRD DAY //

Your letter said that You were leaving
But You didn't know how long
I have never stopped believing
That one day You would return
And though the waiting is the hardest
Part of everything I do
I do confess it's getting better
Knowing I will be with You

It's alright
It's okay
I won't worry 'bout tomorrow
For it brings me one more day
Closer than I was to You

Now the question isn't "will You?"
What I want to know is when
If it's one day or a million
I will wait for You 'til then
So I'm holding on to Your words
And the promises You've made
There is not one You have broken
There's not one I didn't take

Your letter said that You were leaving
But You didn't know how long
I will never stop believing
I know one day You will return

/// TRUE HOPE ///

BETHANY STEWART

What do you look forward to? Is there anything you find yourself thinking about and anticipating almost constantly? On this side of Heaven, we can spend lots of time looking forward to earthly things: "I can't wait until . . . I'm out of school . . . I get married . . . I find my ideal job . . . I can live comfortably." The list is potentially infinite.

Looking forward to good things is not a problem, but worrying about them is. In the Sermon on the Mount, Jesus reminds us of the futility of worry: "Can all your worries add a single moment to your life? Of course not" (Matthew 6:27). As Christians we have much to look forward to.

Have you ever longed for Heaven? It's easy to get so caught up in the things right in front of our faces that we forget Jesus' promise to come back. What should be a growing hope filled with anticipation often is reduced to a passing thought whenever we're reminded of death. What makes this happen?

One contributing factor is that we don't know when Jesus is coming back. It's been over two thousand years since Christ left earth, and he has yet to return. Many have tried to predict Christ's return, but they've all been wrong. This shouldn't be a surprise. When he was leaving the disciples, Jesus said, "It is not for you to know the times or dates the Father has set by his own authority" (Acts 1:7, *NIV*). It could be today or it could be fifty years from now or more.

It's also hard to look forward to something that we don't completely understand. But God can use our lack of comprehension to help build our character and strengthen our trust in him. "For if you already have something, you don't need to hope for it. But if we look forward to something we don't have yet, we must wait patiently and confidently" (Romans 8:24, 25).

It really comes down to looking at what Jesus promised and living and trusting in him. "So I'm holding on to Your words and the promises You've made. There is not one You have broken." He is trustworthy. He *is* coming back. And he is our one *true* hope.

PRAYER FOCUS

Ask God to help your heart and mind to focus more on eternity and his purposes instead of your own worries.

/// YOUR CUE ///

Read John 14 and reflect on Jesus' teachings about his return. How does that impact the way you look at time?

_____

_____

_____

_____

_____

_____

_____

_____

_____

_____

_____

What keeps you from thinking about Jesus' return? How can you live in a way that helps you anticipate Heaven?

_____

_____

_____

_____

_____

_____

_____

_____

_____

_____

Have you seen God keep his Word? What keeps you from trusting in his promises?

_____

_____

_____

_____

_____

_____

_____

_____

_____

_____

LORD REIGN IN ME

// **BRENTON BROWN** //

Over all the earth
You reign on high
Every mountain stream
Every sunset sky
But my one request
Lord, my only aim
Is that You reign in me again

Lord, reign in me
Reign in Your power
Over all my dreams
In my darkest hour
You are the Lord
Of all I am
So won't You reign in me again

Over every thought
Over every word
May my life reflect
The beauty of my Lord
'Cause You mean more to me
Than any earthly thing
So won't You reign in me again

/// OVER ALL ///

BETHANY STEWART

t he earth is the Lord's, and everything in it" (Psalm 24:1).

As creator of the earth and universe, God has inherent authority. Nature acknowledges this without hesitation (Psalm 66:4). Humans, however, are a different story. By God's design, every person has the ability to recognize or reject God's rule over his life. The word *reign* isn't used much in today's democratic, self-sufficient culture—it indicates a type of royal or absolute authority. To be under another's reign involves far more than doing a few favors for that person. It is allowing someone else to have control over your life.

Although each person has a choice to submit to or reject God, God's authority remains constant. God will be praised—if not by people, then by inanimate objects. As Jesus rode into Jerusalem and the crowds of disciples began to worship him, the Pharisees asked Jesus to stop them. Rather than asking them to be quiet, Jesus told the Pharisees that if the people stopped worshiping him, "the stones will cry out" (Luke 19:40, *NIV*).

Regardless of our reactions, God is worthy and sovereign and powerful. There are times when our individual lives are so busy, it seems like more than one person can handle. But God is never overwhelmed, not even by the most intense circumstances we may face. What an amazing thing to give our whole lives to a God who is so mighty!

And so we can offer God our whole lives—but not out of obligation. God desires us to joyfully present ourselves to him, and we can do this because of the kind of king he is. Rather than a dictator or a tyrant, he allows us to become his sons and daughters. Romans 8:17 tells us that "if we are children, then we are heirs—heirs of God and co-heirs with Christ, if indeed we share in his sufferings in order that we may also share in his glory" *(NIV)*. It is definitely an honor to serve a king as loving and generous as he is.

Pray for God to be glorified and have authority over specific areas of your life. Pray that he would reveal areas that need to come under his control rather than your own.

/// YOUR CUE ///

Take the concept of surrendering in this song and write new lines.

Examples:

Lord, reign in the thoughts I have today

Lord, reign in my interactions with people today

Lord, reign in my relationship with _____ today

Lord, reign in the way that I work today

Lord, reign in _____

_____

_____

_____

_____

_____

_____

_____

_____

_____

_____

_____

What's one area of your life that needs to be surrendered to God?

_____
_____
_____
_____
_____
_____
_____
_____
_____
_____

Read Psalm 68:32-35 and reflect on God's power.

_____
_____
_____
_____
_____
_____
_____
_____
_____
_____
_____

MAKE MY LIFE A PRAYER

// **PERFORMED BY KEITH GREEN** //

Make my life a prayer to You
I want to do what You want me to
No empty words and no white lies
No token prayers, no compromise
I want to shine the light You gave
Through Your Son You sent to save us
From ourselves and our despair
It comforts me to know You're really there

I want to thank You now
For being patient with me
Oh it's so hard to see
When my eyes are on me
I guess I'll have to trust
And just believe what You say
Oh You're coming again
Coming to take me away

I want to die and let You give
Your life to me so I might live
And share the hope You gave to me
The love that set me free
I want to tell the world out there
You're not some fable or fairy tale
That I made up inside my head
You're God, the Son
You've risen from the dead

/// YOUR LIFE IN ME ///

BETHANY STEWART

hen Jesus said to the disciples, 'If any of you wants to be my follower, you must put aside your selfish ambition, shoulder your cross, and follow me. If you try to keep your life for yourself, you will lose it. But if you give up your life for me, you will find true life'" (Matthew 16:24, 25).

Do you want to die? That might seem like an odd question to some, but the Christian life requires us to die to our own sinful nature so that we can have life in Christ. Sound strange? It's definitely not natural—but it's necessary. Thankfully God shows his love and patience through Jesus' death. However, as Jesus said to his disciples, accepting his grace should bring about a big difference in the way we look at our lives.

Dying to our own selfish desires is telling Jesus: "I want to do what You want me to." How many times have you prayed that, only to find yourself doing things you shouldn't? Going through the motions but not living authentically, making small compromises that only you know about, or giving in to temptation? Our best intentions often end up frustrated; we find ourselves giving less than we know God deserves. Rather than glorifying God with our lives, we focus on ourselves.

Human beings are selfish—some more than others, but it's our nature to put ourselves first. We see our own needs more often than anyone else's. Unfortunately that tendency isn't the best. Imagine trying to do anything productive while looking at yourself in a mirror. Unless you're getting ready for the day, it's hard to accomplish much of anything. Rather than looking at ourselves, we need to look to Christ, "the author and perfecter of our faith" (Hebrews 12:2, *NIV*) because "it's so hard to see when my eyes are on me."

When we take the focus off ourselves, we see opportunities from a different perspective. It's all about giving glory to God and giving our lives to be a part of something much bigger than ourselves.

So if we die to ourselves, what do we live for? "But my life is worth nothing unless I use it for doing the work assigned me by the Lord Jesus—the work of telling others the Good News about God's wonderful kindness and love" (Acts 20:24). There is no more fulfilling way to live than to live surrendered to Christ. "I want to die and let You give Your life to me, so I might live and share the hope You gave to me, the love that set me free."

PRAYER FOCUS

Talk honestly to God about how you want your life to be lived for him.

/// YOUR CUE ///

What part of your life needs to die to Christ? (your priorities, your plans for life, the way you spend your time, etc.)

_____

_____

_____

_____

_____

_____

_____

_____

Take some time to read through the lyrics to "Make My Life a Prayer."
What parts are your prayer and what parts need to be your prayer?

_____

_____

_____

_____

_____

_____

_____

_____

_____

_____

_____

More Scriptures for reflection: Luke 14:25-35; Galatians 2:20;
Philippians 2:1-11.

_____

_____

_____

_____

_____

_____

_____

_____

_____

_____

_____

SOMEWHERE

// PERFORMED BY RICH MULLINS //

Somewhere
Between the lost and the found
We're all hanging empty
Empty and upside down
But I'm hanging on
Though the fall may tempt me
And I believe in the dawn
Though I tremble in the night

Somewhere
Amidst these ins and these outs
There's a fine line of purpose
I follow even now
Through the haze of despair
That confuses and hurts us
I look to see that You're there
And I run toward Your light

Somewhere
Beyond these reasons and feelings
Somewhere
Beyond the passion and fatigue
I know You're there
And that Your Spirit is leading me
Somewhere
Beyond all this

Someday
Now I don't know when
But I know that You're coming
You're coming back again
And the earth will burn away
And the sky fill with thundering
As it announces the day
That has finally arrived

Somewhere
While the time is still now
While we're still hanging empty
Empty and upside down
But I'm hanging on
With all that is in me
And I'll sing my song
And I'll laugh until I fly

Somewhere
Beyond these reasons and feelings
Somewhere
Beyond the passion and fatigue
I know You're there
And that Your Spirit is leading me
Somewhere
Beyond all this

/// BEYOND ALL THIƧ ///

BETHANY STEWART

there are times when it's hard to see beyond the here and now. The things that seem so important . . . really aren't. The things that *are* most important rarely receive the attention they deserve. We often lose ourselves to the things of this world and shut our eyes on God's light. When you find yourself "hanging empty, empty and upside down," running in circles, or about to drop . . . believe it or not, the most productive thing to do is to focus on the eternal.

"I believe in the dawn though I tremble in the night"—

> When you are worn out, trust that Jesus is preparing a place for you to rest forever.
>
> When you find yourself dependent on this world, trust that Jesus will meet your every need.
>
> When life appears purposeless, trust that Jesus has given you a mission and that he's coming back.
>
> When you have been hurt, trust that there will be a time when it won't hurt anymore.
>
> When your emotions are ruling your life, trust that Jesus left his Word and his Spirit.

At the end of the day—regardless of your present circumstances— Jesus is victorious. We can rest in his promises: "I have told you all this so that you may have peace in me. Here on earth you will have many trials and sorrows. But take heart, because I have overcome the world" (John 16:33).

"We are pressed on every side by troubles, but we are not crushed and broken. We are perplexed, but we don't give up and quit. We are hunted down, but God never abandons us. We get knocked down, but we get up again and keep going" (2 Corinthians 4:8, 9).

"That is why we never give up. Though our bodies are dying, our spirits are being renewed every day. For our present troubles are quite small and won't last very long! Yet they produce for us an immeasurably great glory that will last forever! So we don't look at the troubles we can see right now; rather, we look forward to what we have not yet seen. For the troubles we see will soon be over, but the joys to come will last forever" (2 Corinthians 4:16-18).

PRAYER FOCUS

Pray that God would help you see beyond the here and now of this world. Ask God to direct your focus to that which is eternal and to give you rest through his promises.

/// YOUR CUE ///

In your life today, what is the "all this" mentioned in the song?

_____

_____

_____

_____

_____

_____

_____

_____

_____

_____

_____

What can you do to follow the Spirit's leading to get past it?

_____

_____

_____

_____

_____

_____

_____

_____

_____

_____

DRAW ME
TO YOUR THRONE

// PERFORMED BY DOUG COLLINS //

Father, I want to know You
But my coward heart is so afraid
To give up its toys
Lord of all, I long to surrender
But this foolish mind wants worldly
   pleasure
Instead of Your joy
So will You lift me to my feet
By the power of Your Son
I may come stumbling
But Lord, I'll still come

Draw me to Your throne
Be Lord of my life
Then will my heart be for You
A pleasing sacrifice
I'll give up all I claim I own
If only You to meet
Then will You use me
As a footstool for your lovely feet
Draw me to Your throne
Be Lord of my life

Father, I want to know you
But my callous heart is still convinced
That it knows what's best
Lord of all, I long to surrender
But my selfish mind hoards worldly
   habits
That keep me from Your rest
So will You lift me to my feet
By the power of Your Son
I may come stumbling
But Lord, I'll still come

Root from me these weeds
I've cherished for so long
Then shall you dwell here without
A rival in Your home
And come and be my light
The beacon of my soul
Then shall I know no more darkness,
   loneliness or cold
Draw me to Your throne
Draw me to Your throne
Draw me to Your throne
Be Lord of my life

/// TREMBLING BOLDNE// ///

CARESS ABERCROMBIE

Stumbling toward God is not my idea of how my spiritual life should be. I expect much more out of myself. I want to be brave, bold, and fearless—like a Christian superhero. But the reality is just the opposite. If I come to God at all, I come stumbling. If I realize who he truly is, I tremble. God never intended us to be perfect. Had he expected that, he never would have given Adam guidelines in the garden for what was acceptable and not acceptable; there would have been no need. No, he didn't create us perfect. He created us to be connected with him, to be loved, and to love in return.

John 15:5 tells us that apart from Jesus, we can do nothing. It is his grace that allows us to remain in him. But it is our pride and fear that keep us from truly surrendering. Our pride tells us that our perception of the universe, based on the tangibles of earthly living, is more true than the seemingly surreal reality of God. Pride is sin. But fear is frailty. Fear is a natural response to the immenseness of God. But remaining in fear denies the reality of grace. Our fear keeps us bound in our temporal beliefs because the alternative is mind-blowing.

Our minds cannot truly comprehend all that God is. And that's OK. Psalm 131 says, "LORD, my heart is not proud; my eyes are not haughty. I don't concern myself with matters too great or awesome for me. But I have stilled and quieted myself, just as a small child is quiet with its mother. Yes, like a small child is my soul within me. O Israel, put your hope in the LORD—now and always." The psalmist realized both the nature of the throne of God and his place in relation to it. The throne is the comfort and safety of a mother's arms, and we are at our best when we accept the safety—when we rest and live in love.

/// YOUR CUE ///

What keeps you from coming fully to God? Are you a perfectionist who can't accept grace? Were you denied love and therefore can't trust? Are you prone to a busy do-it-yourself lifestyle that doesn't include needing God?

_____

_____

_____

_____

_____

_____

_____

_____

What do you fear? What do you think it means to fear God?

_____

_____

_____

_____

_____

_____

_____

_____

_____

_____

What do you think of when you think of the throne of God? There are many images, from the mother's breast to the fiery images of Revelation. What different images remind you of God's love? power? justice? mercy?

_____

_____

_____

_____

_____

_____

_____

_____

_____

_____

HOW COULD I ASK FOR MORE

// PERFORMED BY CINDY MORGAN //

There's nothing like the warmth of a summer afternoon
Waking to the sunlight, and being cradled by the moon
Catching fireflies at night
Building castles in the sand
Kissing Mama's face goodnight
Holding Daddy's hand
Thank you, Lord, how could I ask for more

Running barefoot through the grass
A little hide and go seek
Being so in love, that you can hardly eat
Dancing in the dark, when there's no one else around
Being bundled 'neath the covers, watching snow
Fall to the ground
Thank you, Lord, how could I ask for more

So many things I thought would bring me happiness
Some dreams that are realities today
Such an irony the things that mean the most to me
Are the memories that I've made along the way
So if there's anything I've learned
From this journey I am on
Simple truths will keep you going
Simple love will keep you strong
Cause there are questions without answers
Flames that never die
Heartaches we go through are often blessings in disguise
So thank you, Lord, oh thank you, Lord,
How could I ask for more

THE CURRENCY OF ETERNITY

CARESS ABERCROMBIE

ecclesiastes ponders the meaninglessness of life. Much philosophizing and much learning preceded its penning. Solomon was granted wisdom like no other man. And yet, his conclusion on life: it's meaningless. Our only solace is to fear and obey God (Ecclesiastes 12:13) and enjoy life (Ecclesiastes 3:12, 13).

When human life began, Adam's relationship with God was one of joy. His duties were gratifying, and his relationships were fulfilling. He truly needn't have asked for more. Yet he did.

Why do *we* ask for more? Why are we dissatisfied with God's provision?

It is our sinful nature that asks for more than we need. It is our pride that convinces us that we can find fulfillment through anything besides the things of God. Pleasing God and enjoying our lives rest on contentment, which is being satisfied with what God has given.

God created family to be the greatest source of tangible enjoyment this side of Heaven. Our closest human relationships are a picture of how God loves us and relates to us. We quickly realize that pride and greed get us nowhere with the ones we love, and that their love cannot be bought. Though money is the currency of earth, unconditional love is the currency of eternity.

Nowhere in our lives are our loyalties more polarized than in the area of money. To live the American dream, you must pursue wealth. To live for God, you must hold wealth only loosely. Our culture values the sinful nature rather than pleasing God. Few cultural limits are put on the greed that displeases God.

That is not to say that you must be destitute to be a Christian. Solomon was granted vast wealth as a blessing from God precisely because he chose not to pursue it. But what you must do is pursue relationships over the things of this world and revel in the abundance of what God has given you.

PRAYER FOCUS

Thank God for what you have been given. Repent of greed. Ask God to help you identify areas in which you are choosing wealth over relationships.

/// YOUR CUE ///

Do you ever try to fill a void (be it loneliness, hurt, anxiety, etc.) with material items?

_____

_____

_____

_____

_____

_____

_____

_____

_____

_____

_____

What are some practical ways you can practice choosing quality relationships over money and cultural norms of spending?

_____

_____

_____

_____

_____

_____

_____

_____

_____

_____

_____

JOY IN THE JOURNEY

// PERFORMED BY MICHAEL CARD //

There is a joy in the journey
There's a light we can love on the way
There is a wonder and wildness to life
And freedom for those who obey

And all those who seek it shall find it
A pardon for all who believe
Hope for the hopeless and sight for the blind

To all who've been born in the Spirit
And who share incarnation with Him
Who belong to eternity stranded in time
And weary of struggling with sin

Forget not the hope that's before you
And never stop counting the cost
Remember the hopelessness when you were lost

There is a joy in the journey
There's a light we can love on the way
There is a wonder and wildness to life
And freedom for those who obey

And freedom for those who obey . . .

FREEDOM
/// IN OBEDIENCE? ///

CARESS ABERCROMBIE

I n the south of Russia lies a small province, not much bigger than the state of New Jersey, which, in the past fifteen years, has seen unbelievable carnage. Chechnya refuses the rule of Russia yet cannot rule itself—and has thus become a modern example of an anarchic system. There is no established or enforced rule of law. Terrorism and tribal warfare are far more common than justice or cooperation. Consequently there is no safety. Only fear. No rules. Yet no freedom.

Theoretically, we realize the key to our safety and governmental stability is in a strong system of rules and their enforcement. Practically, however, many of us want as few rules as possible. We prefer freedom and individuality to a rigid legal structure.

The same is also true in regard to our relationship with God. Any joy, light, wonder, and wildness we might find temporally is most abundantly and fully found within God's laws, which are established eternally.

Psalm 119 revels in God's laws. It's easy to revel in love, beauty, and comfort. But to revel in law seems somehow counterintuitive. The psalmist loved God's commands because he knew he was not made for the deception, intrigue, manipulation, and one-upmanship of earthly institutions. God honors truth, mercy, and justice while our peers often demand results and good presentation without much thought to the underlying issues of human friendship and character.

Choosing obedience to God's law results in joy. Joy does not cloak circumstances in superficial exuberance. Rather it chooses to see circumstances in light of eternity. Holocaust survivor Viktor Frankl stated it this way: "Emotion, which is suffering, ceases to be suffering as soon as we form a clear and precise picture of it."

Joy disarms pain, fear, rage, and all other manifestations unique to a depraved world simply by reminding us that one day this world will fall. But we need not fall with it—we've been given a "light we can love" on this journey.

PRAYER FOCUS

Pray that you will grow in love and passion for God's truth and for following his perfect guidelines.

/// YOUR CUE ///

Have you ever reveled in God's laws, thanking him for boundaries and guidelines? Praise him for his laws.

_____

_____

_____

_____

_____

_____

_____

_____

_____

_____

Is there an area in your life in which you aren't obeying God? Asking God for forgiveness and restoration is not something we outgrow as Christians; it is part of who we are and how we relate to God.

_____

_____

_____

_____

_____

_____

_____

_____

_____

_____

What is something you can do this week to choose joy over defeat? You can choose your attitude. Think of a few ways you can remind yourself to look at life through God's eyes (the big picture).

_____

_____

_____

_____

_____

_____

_____

_____

_____

_____

PIECE OF GLASS

// PERFORMED BY CAEDMON'S CALL //

Can't believe that I did it again
Wake me up from this nightmare
'Cause this monster is filling me up
filling me out

Every day I live a bit less; one night
leads to another
Even if I went back they would recognize
me or criticize me

Who are you that lies when you stare in
my face
Telling me that I'm just a trace of the
person I once was
'Cause I just can't tell if you're telling
the truth or a lie
On you I just can't rely. After all you're
just a piece of glass

Still this nightmare's all mine, when I
call him he answers
I can tell him when to come, when to
stay
Sometimes I'm weaker than he is, is he
just letting me win
He can tell me when to come, when to
stay

Who are you that lies when you stare in
my face
Telling me that I'm just a trace of the
person I once was
'Cause I just can't tell if you're telling
the truth or a lie
On you I just can't rely. After all you're
just a piece of glass

Don't talk, listen
Hold me tighter
Stay with me just for a while
Until the sun shines stay with me
Just give me one more day

Who are you that cries when you stare in
my face
Telling me that I'm just a trace of the
person I once was
'Cause we're not the same, you're just a
picture of me
You're gone as soon as I leave; you've
lived my life for me
And you're no more than a piece of glass
You're no more than just a piece of glass

WHAT CAN SEPARATE US?

CARESS ABERCROMBIE

Sin separates us from God. That is its power. Life apart from God is death. Thus sin leads to death. Why does sin separate us from God? God is just. He cannot accommodate what is less than holy. His justice does not change and therefore renders sin absolute . . . black and white.

We know God's grace is sufficient. However, our own ability to extend grace to ourselves is inadequate. Hence sin also separates us from God because of our shame. God has blessed us with a conscience that produces feelings of guilt when we've violated his laws. But a conscience, like our frail bodies, can be damaged. A damaged conscience can result in feeling little to no guilt when sinning—or it can result in false guilt and immobilizing shame. In the latter case, we choose wallowing in guilt instead of turning to God for forgiveness, healing, and restoration.

Should we be grieved by our sin as God is grieved? Yes, unequivocally. But in our shame, we must turn toward God instead of away, as he is our only hope for transformation. Take the woman caught in adultery in John 8:1-11. Her guilt was clear. But Jesus said, "Neither do I condemn you. . . . Go now and leave your life of sin" (John 8:11, *NIV*).

How could Jesus say that to her? What was he thinking? How could he be sure she would stop sinning? Wasn't he worried that she would go back to her immoral ways and therefore waste his good efforts? What if she became flippant about grace? And yet . . . Jesus was always right. He always kept his perspective and response in perfect balance. He was always pure. He never compromised his integrity. And he was never, ever casual about sin.

Could it be that if we were to truly encounter the grace of Jesus, we couldn't help but be transformed? If we would accept the reality that Jesus releases us from the death that we deserve, we would realize that something that is freely given is never attached to a lot of stipulations. It is simply given out of love.

And what better response to a woman so full of shame, so strikingly guilty, than for Jesus to say, "I don't condemn you. Go. You're forgiven." How could she not be changed?

PRAYER FOCUS

Seek God's truth in prayer. Ask him for discernment. You can never be too repentant; if you feel guilty or shameful, turn toward God. He will be faithful to forgive and to restore.

/// YOUR CUE ///

What do you think of Jesus' response to the woman? What would the Pharisees have thought? his disciples? the woman?

_____

_____

_____

_____

_____

_____

_____

_____

_____

_____

_____

What are the things that fill you with shame? Ask for God's forgiveness and pray that he will help you to forgive yourself.

_____

_____

_____

_____

_____

_____

_____

_____

_____

_____

Do you have someone who can help you know what is truly sinful and what you're experiencing false guilt about? Practice accountability with a friend or counselor who can give you some outside perspective.

_____

_____

_____

_____

_____

_____

_____

_____

_____

WHO AM I?

// PERFORMED BY CASTING CROWNS //

Who am I?
That the Lord of all the earth
Would care to know my name
Would care to feel my hurt
Who am I?
That the Bright and Morning Star
Would choose to light the way
For my ever wandering heart

Not because of who I am
But because of what You've done
Not because of what I've done
But because of who You are

Who am I?
That the eyes that see my sin
Would look on me with love
And watch me rise again
Who am I?
That the voice that calmed the sea
Would call out through the rain
And calm the storm in me

Not because of who I am
But because of what You've done
Not because of what I've done
But because of who You are

I am a flower quickly fading
Here today and gone tomorrow
A wave tossed in the ocean
A vapor in the wind
Still You hear me when I'm calling
Lord, You catch me when I'm falling
And You've told me who I am
I am Yours, I am Yours

I am Yours
Whom shall I fear?
Whom shall I fear?
'Cause I am Yours
I am Yours

/// GLIMP/E/ OF ETERNITY ///

CARESS ABERCROMBIE

a friend died this weekend. It is not fair that his flower faded too early. It is not fair that youth has been shattered. It is not fair that dreams will never find fulfillment. It is not fair that hope and promise and joy have been relegated to the category of mere memory.

And yet, astoundingly, God remains the same. He has not changed, though we have. Three days ago we trusted in his faithfulness and justice. To trust less now would show our own frailty, not the Father's. He does not love us less for our grief, anger, or incomprehension. No, in our pain, he could not love us more.

Beyond the questions of "How could this happen?" and "How do we move on?" the essence of eternity remains unchanged, though our perception has been fundamentally altered. Our eyes are ripped open to the reality that has always been true but has been unseen by us—we are mere caricatures of strength. We are frail. We are easily undone.

The fundamental nature of our identity is and always will be inextricably linked to who God is. But we rarely glimpse the full weight of what this means. Intellectually, when we come to Christ, we know that our only power, our only worth, and our only utility come through him. Yet, perhaps by his grace, we do not understand what that will cost. And when we experience the pain of that sacrifice, we are utterly shaken.

This being taken aback by eternity comes because we do not know how to interact with it. In many ways God is more mysterious than ever. We are often reduced to awed silence because we know that any explanation, any justification, any comfort we find in God/eternity is merely a fraction of the whole of who God is.

We find it incomprehensible to navigate eternity and temporal life at the same time. Jesus was the only human ever to master this art. He mastered it because he lived in eternity before he lived in time and therefore had the thing we most lack: perspective.

Did perspective make Jesus' personal experience of death more bearable? Perhaps intellectually. But he, like us, was not solely an intellectual being. In fact, his very perfection made him unable to separate emotion from logic—they were held in perfect balance. Jesus felt more deeply than we will because of his perfection and because he felt the weight of all the sin of the world. Because he knows us intimately, he loves us. And that love is our only hope.

PRAYER FOCUS

Pray that God will give you an eternal perspective. Pray for courage and peace as you look beyond earthly values and time constraints.

/// YOUR CUE ///

What reminds you of your dependence on God? Does sacrificial giving? fasting? reading a particular author? Make those things that draw you outside of your day-to-day, complacent, earthly living a regular part of connecting with God.

_____

_____

_____

_____

_____

_____

_____

_____

How would you finish the sentence, "I am_____"? How would you finish the sentence if you didn't know God? Are you sometimes tempted to forget who you are and live according to the latter?

_____

_____

_____

_____

_____

_____

_____

_____

_____

_____

What is your favorite characteristic of God? What is the attribute that makes you feel most connected to him?

_____

_____

_____

_____

_____

_____

_____

_____

_____

_____

JOYFUL, JOYFUL, WE ADORE THEE

// PERFORMED BY LAURYN HILL //

Joyful, joyful, we adore Thee,
God of glory, Lord of love;
Hearts unfold like flowers before Thee
opening to the sun above.
Melt the clouds of sin and sadness;
drive the dark of doubt away;
Giver of immortal gladness,
fill us with the light of day!

All Thy works with joy surround Thee,
earth and heaven reflect Thy rays,
Stars and angels sing around Thee,
center of unbroken praise.
Field and forest, vale and mountain,
flowery meadow, flashing sea,
Singing bird and flowing fountain
call us to rejoice in Thee.

Thou art giving and forgiving,
ever blessing, ever blessed,
Wellspring of the joy of living,
ocean depth of happy rest!
Thou our Father, Christ our Brother,
all who live in love are Thine;
Teach us how to love each other,
lift us to the joy divine.

Mortals, join the happy chorus,
which the morning stars began;
Father love is reigning o'er us,
brother love binds man to man.
Ever singing, march we onward,
victors in the midst of strife,
Joyful music leads us Sunward
in the triumph song of life.

Words by Henry Van Dyke. Public Domain.

/// HEARTS UNFOLDED ///

CHRIS IGNIZIO

his hymn was written while Henry J. Van Dyke was gazing upon the beauty of the mountains of Massachusetts. There is something to be said for experiencing the presence of God in the midst of his creation. To sit in the depths of a beautiful valley, or look down from the heights of a mountain. To stare across an ocean, or up at the stars that shine brighter than all the big city lights in the world. To see such things is an affirmation that there is a God who creates and sustains. And when you reconcile that with the knowledge that that same God loves you and me more than anything else formed by his hands, the only reasonable response for us is to be filled with joy.

My favorite passage of Scripture is Psalm 30:5: "Weeping may remain for a night, but rejoicing comes in the morning" *(NIV).* This life certainly has no shortage of heartache and pain. And to be honest, it takes work to be joyful. But the opportunities to do so are unending because our Father has given us this life as a gift, and he expects us to be full of joy over it.

This song is about those times of joy, like when we first asked Christ into our lives. Do you remember when you first allowed him to invade your world? I remember having joy in the midst of the uncertainty of my new relationship with him. While I had no idea what he would do with my life, I knew that my life would be forever changed. This song is about those times when we allow our hearts to "unfold like flowers before Thee," so that he can fill them up. Sometimes he does that with brotherly love that "binds man to man," or with the joy that comes from time with a loved one, or with simple things like a good song or a long drive on a sunny day.

When we become believers, God actually places this joy inside us through his Holy Spirit. These aren't just comforting words; they're truth. We must have the faith that our God can truly "drive the dark of doubt away," or else we will become entombed in darkness. There are two reasons that he has filled us "with the light of day." One is that we were never intended to be enveloped in the darkness that comes from sin. The other is that the world is still stumbling blindly through that same darkness, and he has entrusted us with the light to rescue it so that we might all join "in the triumph song of life."

PRAYER FOCUS

Pray that God would help you live in full awareness of the joy he offers. Pray that he would help you realize all the things he has given you to be joyful over. Pray that others would see the joy you have through Jesus.

/// YOUR CUE ///

Are you truly joyful about being alive and knowing Jesus Christ? Why or why not?

_____

_____

_____

_____

_____

_____

_____

_____

_____

_____

_____

Do others see the "light of day" in you? Would a nonbeliever see something in you that he would want to have?

_____

_____

_____

_____

_____

_____

_____

_____

_____

_____

What is it that fills your life with joy? Do you make time in your life for these things?

_____

_____

_____

_____

_____

_____

_____

_____

_____

_____

MEANT TO LIVE

// PERFORMED BY SWITCHFOOT //

Fumbling his confidence
And wondering why the world has passed him by
Hoping that he's bid for more than arguments
And failed attempts to fly, fly

We were meant to live for so much more
Have we lost ourselves?
Somewhere we live inside
Somewhere we live inside
We were meant to live for so much more
Have we lost ourselves?
Somewhere we live inside

Dreaming about providence
And whether mice or men have second tries
Maybe we've been livin' with our eyes half open
Maybe we're bent and broken, broken

We want more than this world's got to offer
We want more than this world's got to offer
We want more than the wars of our fathers
And everything inside screams for second life, yeah

We were meant to live for so much more
Have we lost ourselves?
We were meant to live for so much more
Have we lost ourselves?
We were meant to live for so much more
Have we lost ourselves?
We were meant to live
We were meant to live

/// LIFE IN EPIC PROPORTION ///

CHRIS IGNIZIO

t is no small thing to die a spiritual death and be raised up again a different being than before. But 2 Corinthians 5:17 tells us that in Christ we have become a "new creation" *(NIV).* Yet we find with terrible frequency that we have not changed all that much from our former selves. Sure, we may have a new intellectual outlook on life. And we may fare better in times of trouble because we treat our Savior as someone obliged to bail us out and comfort us then. Sometimes we even "feel" God—in times of worship or when he speaks to us through his Word.

But if we're honest with ourselves, we may find that we still feel as if "the world has passed [us] by"—our lives are as monotonous and mundane as ever. We experience regret over "failed attempts to fly"— or because we're not even attempting to fly. We mourn the moments we should have seized and a life lived without passion or purpose.

We really were "meant to live for so much more." Our God did not send his Son to such a torturous death so that we would remain "bent and broken," "livin' with our eyes half open." The life he offers is a healed one that is meant to be taken head-on with abandon and fervor. Look at the lives of any of the heroes in the Bible. There are journeys across parted seas and battles won against seemingly impossible odds. Jeremiah 29:11 tells us that God has a plan, hope, and future for each of our lives. We may never find ourselves toe to toe with a giant or walking on water, but any life lived in worship and service of the author of life is an epic.

To truly live is to be in an intimate relationship with our creator, a relationship in which there is love and purpose and work and worship and rejoicing. A life lived for Christ demands a certain "insanity" and recklessness—born not of disregard or irresponsibility, but born of commitment to the will of God and out of the faith that the things that God is about are bigger than we can fathom.

Everything inside us "screams for second life" because we need it. We were designed for it. Anything less would be to slander Christ's sacrifice on the cross. Nothing less is sufficient if we want to light a world that is meant for so much more than it comprehends.

PRAYER FOCUS

Pray that God would help you have the courage and trust to live the life that Jesus died to give you. Pray that he would show you opportunities and desires that he has for you that you may be ignoring or are too afraid to see. And pray that he would help you step out in faith in those areas and that he would draw you closer to him.

/// YOUR CUE ///

How has your life changed since you made Christ your Lord and Savior?

_____
_____
_____
_____
_____
_____
_____

Are you living your life in the fullness found in God's will? If not, what is holding you back?

_____
_____
_____
_____

_____

_____

_____

_____

_____

_____

_____

Is there something that you feel God is calling you to that you're afraid of?

_____

_____

_____

_____

_____

_____

What regrets are you afraid of having, and what can you do to prevent them?

_____

_____

_____

_____

_____

_____

_____

_____

_____

TAKE MY LIFE, AND LET IT BE

// PERFORMED BY CHRIS TOMLIN //

Take my life, and let it be
consecrated, Lord, to Thee.
Take my moments and my days;
let them flow in ceaseless praise.

Take my hands, and let them move
at the impulse of Thy love.
Take my feet, and let them be
swift and beautiful for Thee.

Take my voice, and let me sing
always, only, for my King.
Take my lips, and let them be
filled with messages from Thee.

Take my silver and my gold;
not a mite would I withhold.
Take my intellect, and use
every power as Thou shalt choose.

Take my will, and make it Thine;
it shall be no longer mine.
Take my heart, it is Thine own;
it shall be Thy royal throne.

Take my love, my Lord, I pour
at Thy feet its treasure store.
Take myself, and I will be
ever, only, all for Thee.

Words by H.A. Hendon. Public Domain.

/// BEAUTY OF /URRENDER ///

CHRIS IGNIZIO

he first time I fell in love, I found myself doing strange things that I wouldn't normally do. I did many things simply because they were important to the girl I was in love with. To be honest, I wound up going to church because of her. And eventually as I transitioned from being "in love" with her to actually loving her, *my* life became about *her* life.

When we really love someone, we are able to look past ourselves for the sake of that person because love is sacrificial. The things that are important to them become important to us. We become willing to give ourselves completely to someone because we love him or her.

"Take My Life, and Let It Be" is about this same kind of devotion and surrender to Jesus Christ. It is about loving him so much that our lives become his as a response to his love for us. This is the relationship he longs to have with us: that we exist for him, care about what he cares for, and love the people he loves.

This is where surrender becomes something beautiful for a Christian. When we hand ourselves over to God, it is not just out of duty or obligation, but out of joyous gratitude. When we realize that our lives are only meaningful when lived for God, we begin to realize that there is no lasting impact or satisfaction in living for ourselves. It becomes easier to ask Jesus to "take [our] moments and [our] days." The better we know him, the more deeply we are able to love him, and the more we want to "sing always, only, for [our] King" and long for him to "take [our] heart . . . it is Thine own." Indeed, the entirety of our journey as Christians is to become exclusively his.

Artist-worshiper Chris Tomlin has added a chorus to this classic hymn. The added words are: "Here am I, all of me, take my life, it's all for thee." This attitude of surrender follows Paul's exhortation for sacrifice. In Romans 12:1 Paul writes, "Therefore, I urge you, brothers, in view of God's mercy, to offer your bodies as living sacrifices, holy and pleasing to God—this is your spiritual act of worship" *(NIV)*. By giving him the totality of our lives—our moments and days, our hands and feet, our silver and gold, our intellect and our love—we worship and serve and love our God. We furnish our hearts as the place where he dwells. It's "all for Thee."

PRAYER FOCUS

Pray that God would make your life his. Ask him to reveal the parts of your life that you're holding onto and to help you surrender them. Ask him to show you where your desires conflict with his.

/// YOUR CUE ///

Why is it so difficult for us to give our lives to God? What is it that keeps you from doing this?

_____

_____

_____

_____

_____

_____

_____

_____

_____

_____

What in your life have you not given over or surrendered to God? What do you think would be the result of your surrendering this over to God?

_____

_____

_____

_____

_____

_____

_____

_____

_____

_____

DRAW ME CLOSE

// PERFORMED BY MICHAEL W. SMITH //

Draw me close to You
Never let me go
I lay it all down again
To hear You say that I'm Your friend

You are my desire
No one else will do
Cause nothing else could take Your place,
To feel the warmth of Your embrace
Help me find the way
Bring me back to You

You're all I want
You're all I've ever needed
You're all I want
Help me know You are near

/// OBVIOUSLY IN LOVE ///

CHRISTY BARRITT

"If anyone would come after me, he must deny himself and take up his cross and follow me" (Mark 8:34, *NIV*).

I love music. I rush to get the latest CDs from my favorite artists. I memorize the lyrics and melodies to songs and quietly hum them to myself during the day. When talking to people about the latest concerts and artist news, I could go on and on all day. My passion is obvious to anyone who knows me.

Sometimes I wonder if my passion for Jesus is as obvious. If Jesus were truly my only desire, it would show in my life. I wouldn't neglect my quiet time with him in favor of having other fun, being lazy, or overindulging in work. I would be consumed with telling others about the awesome love of Christ and how it can change them just as it's changed me. If Jesus were my only desire, I'd put my money toward his work, toward helping others who are less fortunate instead of seeing the latest movie or buying the latest fashion trend. If Jesus were my only desire, I wouldn't be distracted by worldly charms that entice me with false promises of fulfillment.

How would your life change if Jesus were truly your only desire? Would you continue to whittle your time away doing things that are of value only on this earth? Or would you do things with an eternal vision, as it says in 2 Corinthians 4:18?

As we get closer to Jesus, our lives will become more and more like his. We can rest assured that Jesus will never let us go. If you feel distant from him, it's because you've moved away. He's always there beside us.

PRAYER FOCUS

Pray that God would help you put aside anything that draws you away from him and help you realize that he's all you need for peace and joy in this life. Ask him to draw you close and mold your desires so that you can seek to serve only him.

/// YOUR CUE ///

Would you truly lay it all down to hear Jesus say that you're his friend?

_____

_____

_____

_____

_____

_____

_____

_____

_____

_____

Is Jesus your desire? Does your life prove it?

_____

_____

_____

_____

_____

_____

_____

_____

_____

_____

People say you can tell where your heart is by where you put your money. Where is your money going?

_____

_____

_____

_____

_____

_____

_____

_____

_____

_____

FREE

// PERFORMED BY GINNY OWENS //

Turnin' molehills into mountains
Makin' big deals out of small ones,
Bearing gifts as if they're burdens,
This is how it's been.
Fear of coming out of my shell,
Too many things I can't do too well,
Afraid I'll try real hard, and I'll fail—
This is how it's been.
Till the day You pounded on my heart's door,
And You shouted joyfully,
"You're not a slave anymore!"

"You're free to dance—
Forget about your two left feet
And you're free to sing—
Even joyful noise is music to Me
You're free to love,
'Cause I've given you My love
And it's made you free."

My mind finds hard to believe
That You became humanity and changed the course of history,
Because You loved me so.
And my heart cannot understand
Why You'd accept me as I am,
But You say You've always had a plan,
And that's all I need to know.
So when I am consumed by what the world will say,
It's then You're singing to me, as You remove my chains—

Free from worry, free from envy and denial
Free to live, free to give, free to smile

/// ƒLAVE TO INƒECURITY ///

CHRISTY BARRITT

or God has not given us a spirit of fear and timidity, but of power, love, and self-discipline" (2 Timothy 1:7).

I knew that God had given me a passion and a talent, but the thought of performing in front of hundreds people made me shudder with fear. What if I messed up? What if I tripped? What if I didn't hit the right note at the end? What if I forgot the words? Doubt consumed me. Instead of treating the talent God had given me as a blessing, I viewed it as a curse because of my own insecurities.

It's easy to let doubt and insecurity overcome us. Satan works hard to make us question Christ's love for us. All too often we become slaves to the insecurities in our lives. But God wants us to be free. He wants us to be so in love with him that nothing else seems important—not how foolish we may look in front of others, not failing in the world's eyes, not fear of being rejected by our peers or family. God wants us to live without fear and timidity. He wants us to live powerful lives, lives fueled by his love and acceptance.

We're each here on earth for a purpose. God has a plan for us, but it's not until we give up ourselves that we'll be able to embrace what Christ wants to do through our lives.

When insecurity threatens to overcome you, let Christ remove those chains that weigh you down. Feel his arms embracing and accepting you right where you are. Remember that he has made us to be free, and when we stay within the confines of his will, we don't have to worry about being defeated. Christ has already won the battle for us.

PRAYER FOCUS

Ask God to help you embrace the gifts that he has blessed you with. Pray that God would free you from the fears that hold you back and that he would help you to fully embrace him.

/// YOUR CUE ///

What insecurities hold you back from fully serving God?

_____

_____

_____

_____

_____

Do you bear any of your gifts as if they were a burden? How can you turn that around? Do you realize when/how this attitude comes on?

_____

_____

_____

_____

_____

_____

_____

_____

_____

_____

Do you find it hard to believe that Jesus died for you? that he accepts you just as you are?

_____

_____

_____

What things chain you and hinder your life? Envy? Worry? Denial?

_____

_____

_____

_____

_____

_____

If you were living a truly free life, what would it look like?

_____

_____

_____

_____

_____

_____

_____

_____

_____

_____

I BELIEVE

// PERFORMED BY WES KING //

I believe
In six days and a rest
God is good
I do confess
I believe
In Adam and Eve
In a tree and a garden
In a snake and a thief

I believe, I believe
I believe in the Word of God
I believe, I believe
'Cause He made me believe

I believe Noah
Built an ark of wood
120 years
No one understood
I believe Elijah never died
Called fire from heaven
On a mountainside

It's been passed down through ages of
    time
Written by hands of men
Inspired by the Lord
His Word will remain to the end

I believe Isaiah
Was a prophet of old
The Lamb was slain
Just as he foretold
I believe Jesus
Was the Word made man
And He died for my sins
And He rose again

/// SOLD OUT FOR CHRIST ///

CHRISTY BARRITT

All Scripture is inspired by God and is useful to teach us what is true and to make us realize what is wrong in our lives. It straightens us out and teaches us to do what is right" (2 Timothy 3:16).

There was a popular slogan in the early nineties that graced bumper stickers, key chains, T-shirts, and posters. It read: "God said it, I believe it, that settles it." I thought it was pretty clever. Then one day a friend of mine shared an interesting observation. He said, "Shouldn't it be, 'God said it, that settles it'?" It made me rethink the clever slogan and realize that my believing what God said had absolutely no impact on its truth. God has been the same throughout time, and his truths haven't changed as human opinion has swayed.

Truth sometimes seems a dying conviction as tolerance is becoming more common. While people are becoming more open to accepting the beliefs of all religions, the fact remains that religions that do not center on Christ are ultimately futile. Jesus said in John 14:6, "I am the way and the truth and the life. No one comes to the Father except through me" *(NIV)*. While there are other religions that may preach peace and love, these values aren't substantial without Jesus.

When you feel your conviction wavering, read through the Bible. Historians have proven time and again the authenticity of the events recorded on those pages. Men have set out to prove Christianity false and come back believers. The bottom line is that the Bible is truth, no matter how man may try to distort it.

A belief is something you hold to so deeply that you would die for it. Do you hold enough conviction to stand up for faith in God, even if it means being ridiculed by others? Do you believe so much in the Word that you cling to its promises and dig deep into the pages so you can learn more and be strengthened?

We should always be ready to give an answer when questioned on our faith. When we put conviction behind what we're saying, it can be a great motivator for others to begin asking questions about the light and love they see through us.

PRAYER FOCUS

Pray that you would hold strong to the truth found in Scripture and clutch the promises God has given. Pray that when others look at you, they see someone grounded in conviction, truth, and love.

/// YOUR CUE ///

Do you believe that the Bible is the perfect Word of God? How does that fact comfort you?

_____

_____

_____

_____

_____

_____

_____

_____

_____

_____

_____

Do you believe that God keeps his promises today, just as he did thousands of years ago?

_____

_____

_____

_____

_____

_____

_____

_____

_____

_____

Which of God's promises do you cling to the most fervently? Why? How has it helped you?

_____

_____

_____

_____

_____

_____

_____

_____

_____

_____

I WILL BE WITH YOU

// PERFORMED BY MARGARET BECKER //

There's a candle in the night
There's a refuge within sight
I, I won't cry
There's a dream that I can hold
There's a hope that I can hope
I, I won't cry

When the sun goes black and the moon goes red
And all the final words have been said
I, I will be with You
When every dream is brought to life
And the hands of time roll back the night
I, I will be with You
I, I'm gonna be with you

I'm gonna be with You,
I'm gonna be with You
I'm gonna be with You,
I won't cry,
I'm gonna be with You
There's a hand that will hold mine and lead me to a better time
I, I won't cry

Nothing can separate us,
Nothing will come between us
I know one day I'm gonna be with You
No power in creation, no mortal complication
Will ever stop me from being with You

THROUGH THICK
///   AND THIN   ///

CHRISTY BARRITT

or God has said, 'I will never fail you. I will never forsake you'"
(Hebrews 13:5).

My mom was fond of reminding my siblings and me that friends and
acquaintances would come and go, but family would always be there
for each other. As a teenager I didn't think she knew what she was
talking about—my world revolved around my friends. We vowed our
friendship with broken necklaces, shared secrets, and scrapbooks of
memories. But it wasn't long after high school that we lost touch. We
made new friends. We moved on.

Despite all the changes in friendships, my family has been there.
Through death and illness, good times and bad, we've stuck together.
Today I know my mother's words are true. Whenever I'm having a hard
time, I know I can depend on my family to help me through to the best
of their ability—but we all fall short.

The Bible tells us in Proverbs 18:24 that there is a friend who sticks
closer than a brother. That friend is Jesus. When we feel lonely and
that there's no one else in the world who cares, Jesus is there. When
everyone else turns against us, God's presence will surround us. When
we feel the night will never end and that darkness will prevail, he
will turn our "mourning into joyful dancing" (Psalm 30:11). He's our
candle, our refuge, our dream, and our hope.

We can rest assured that friends, and even family, will at times let
us down. But God is faithful. He loves us and is there throughout
every circumstance in our lives. He's holding our hands and gently
whispering in our ears that, ultimately, everything will be all right.
Everything will be all right.

PRAYER FOCUS

Ask God to help you be aware of his presence, even when it feels like everyone else has forsaken you. Pray that you would be ready to receive the blessings God promised for your life and that you would feel God's loving arms even on the loneliest days.

/// YOUR CUE ///

Do you ever feel as if God is no longer with you? What causes those times to come about? How do you handle them?

_____

_____

_____

_____

_____

_____

_____

_____

_____

_____

_____

Is there a verse that you cling to when hope feels lost? What is it? Why does it comfort you?

_____

_____

_____

_____

_____

_____

_____

_____

_____

What things get in between you and God? Is there anything in your life right now that separates you from God? A relationship? A habit? A lack of discipline?

_____

_____

_____

_____

_____

_____

_____

_____

_____

_____

TO KNOW YOU

// PERFORMED BY NICHOLE NORDEMAN //

It's well past midnight
And I'm awake with questions that
   won't
Wait for daylight
Separating fact from my imaginary
   fiction
On this shelf of my conviction
I need to find a place
Where You and I come face to face

Thomas needed
Proof that You had really risen
Undefeated
When he placed his fingers
Where the nails once broke Your skin
Did his faith finally begin?
I've lied if I've denied
The common ground I've shared with
   him

And I, I really want to know You
I want to make each day
A different way that I can show You how
I really want to love You
Be patient with my doubt
I'm just tryin' to figure out Your will
And I really want to know You still

Nicodemus
Could not understand how You could
Truly free us
He struggled with the image
Of a grown man born again
We might have been good friends
'Cause sometimes I still question, too
How easily we come to You

No more campin' on the porch of
   indecision
No more sleepin' under stars of apathy
And it might be easier to dream
But dreamin's not for me

/// FACING YOUR DOUBTS ///

CHRISTY BARRITT

"t hen he said to Thomas, 'Put your finger here and see my hands. Put your hand into the wound in my side. Don't be faithless any longer. Believe!'" (John 20:27).

Life had been easy. Nothing had really happened to test my faith, and so I merrily went along my way, thinking I was strong. Then, in one year, the tests poured down. My father became terminally ill. A young friend, not even out of high school yet, died unexpectedly. Another friend, in the midst of living out the dreams he worked so hard for, was diagnosed with a brain tumor. My perfect little life was shattered, and suddenly I didn't feel as strong as I had supposed I was.

At first my doubts were coupled with guilt—I couldn't be a *real* Christian and experience doubt. I was weak and unworthy of being called a Christian as I questioned God's existence and wondered where he was in the midst of all of this. Hurt and pain overcame me, and I didn't know what to do with my grief. So I blamed God. I questioned him. I begged him to give me understanding.

Understanding didn't come easily. As I talked to a good friend, he told me that everyone I knew to have a strong faith had gone through a season of doubt, acknowledged it, wrestled with it, and came out stronger in the end. It was a process of being refined, as written about in Zechariah 13:9.

I thought of the story of Job in the Bible. I remembered all the afflictions he endured and how he handled the pain. Despite all of his hardships, he still clung to God. But at the same time, he wasn't afraid to ask hard questions. He wasn't afraid to curse the day he was born. He said to his wife, "Should we accept only good things from the hand of God and never anything bad?" (Job 2:10).

Oftentimes, doubts come out of hard times when we ask God, "Why?"

God is still Lord in the good and bad times though. We can battle our doubt by getting to know God better, by digging into his Word, and by striving to be like him.

/// YOUR CUE ///

How do you deal with doubt? Do you talk to God about it?

_____

_____

_____

_____

_____

_____

_____

_____

Do you desire to truly know God? Do you search the Word to go deeper than what you learned growing up in Sunday school?

_____

_____

_____

_____

_____

Do you relate to Thomas? How does it make you feel? Ashamed? Comforted?

_____

_____

_____

_____

_____

If you've come through a season of doubt, what made you realize that God is real and loving?

_____

_____

_____

_____

_____

Read the story of Nicodemus from John 3. Are you like Nicodemus in any ways? Do you find it hard to believe that faith can free us?

_____

_____

_____

_____

ABOVE ALL

// PERFORMED BY MICHAEL W. SMITH //

Above all powers, above all kings
Above all nature and all created things
Above all wisdom and all the ways of man
You were there before the world began

Above all kingdoms, above all thrones
Above all wonders the world has ever known
Above all wealth and treasures of the earth
There's no way to measure what You're worth

Crucified
Laid behind the stone
You lived to die
Rejected and alone
Like a rose
Trampled on the ground
You took the fall
And thought of me
Above all

/// THE VALUE OF JESUS ///

CHRISTY BARRITT

"The one who comes from above is above all" (John 3:31, *NIV*).

My guitar was my first big purchase once I started earning a real income. When I laid eyes on it, it was love at first sight. Several years later, I still clean it and change its strings and take every precaution to keep it safe and out of harm. I'm picky about whom I let play it because I don't want my instrument to be damaged. Some might say I'm obsessed, and I'm inclined to agree. I value my guitar, and because of that, I act accordingly.

Jesus is more precious than any possession we'll ever have here on earth. Yet, as prized as he is, his beauty is often trampled upon. We neglect the values explained in his Word in favor of a worldly mindset. We're ashamed to say his name in reverence for fear of ridicule. We forget how much he loves us and hurry on with our days without acknowledging his presence in our lives. We've taken something beautiful and cast it aside.

It says in John 3:30 that "he must become greater; I must become less" *(NIV)*. Because we value Christ and our relationship with him, because he is the first and last, the beginning and the end, we must make our own desires secondary to him. When we do this, all of the other aspects of our lives will fall into place. When we put Jesus in his rightful place—above all—we'll receive the peace that Christ gives to those who love and follow him. Remember that Jesus is greater than anything this world has to offer—success, popularity, wealth, or knowledge. He thought of us when he took the fall, and living our lives for him is the least we can do in return.

/// YOUR CUE ///

What things do you put above God? Do they satisfy you in the end?

_____

_____

_____

_____

_____

_____

_____

_____

_____

_____

_____

_____

How can you put God above everything else in your life? What are some ways you can show this and make it evident in your daily walk?

_____

_____

_____

_____

_____

_____

_____

_____

_____

_____

_____

What possession do you value most? Do you value Christ even more?

_____

_____

_____

_____

_____

_____

_____

_____

_____

_____

_____

_____

COME, THOU FOUNT

// PERFORMED BY DAVID CROWDER //

Come, Thou Fount of every blessing,
Tune my heart to sing Thy grace;
Streams of mercy, never ceasing,
Call for songs of loudest praise.
Teach me some melodious sonnet,
Sung by flaming tongues above.
Praise the mount! I'm fixed upon it,
Mount of Thy redeeming love.

Here I raise my Ebenezer;
Hither by Thy help I'm come;
And I hope, by Thy good pleasure,
Safely to arrive at home.
Jesus sought me when a stranger,
Wandering from the fold of God;
He, to rescue me from danger,
Interposed His precious blood.

O to grace how great a debtor
Daily I'm constrained to be!
Let Thy goodness, like a fetter,
Bind my wandering heart to Thee.
Prone to wander, Lord, I feel it,
Prone to leave the God I love;
Here's my heart, O take and seal it,
Seal it for Thy courts above.

O that day when freed from sinning,
I shall see Thy lovely face;
Clothed then in blood washed linen
How I'll sing Thy sovereign grace;
Come, my Lord, no longer tarry,
Take my ransomed soul away;
Send thine angels now to carry
Me to realms of endless day.

Words by Robert Robinson. Public Domain.

/// YOUR EBENEZER ///

DOUG HARTLEY

While I was growing up, I enjoyed many of the hymns we sang in church. There were a few, however, that I found pretty confusing. The second verse of "Come, Thou Fount" would have to be near the top of my list of most perplexing lines in a hymn: "Here I raise my Ebenezer; hither by Thy help I'm come." What? Ebenezer who? Why is he being raised? It was years before I unraveled the meaning of this mysterious "Ebenezer."

The origin of this name is found in 1 Samuel 7:12. The verse comes from a section of Scripture in which the Philistines were harassing the Israelites. The Israelites cried out to God for help against the violent attacks of their enemies, and the Lord sent a severe thunderstorm that threw the Philistines into a panic, thereby allowing the Israelites to pursue and rout their aggressors. It was at this point that Samuel, the Israelite leader, raised a stone to give God credit for their triumph. Samuel called this monument *Ebenezer,* which means "stone of help."

This hymn describes Robert Robinson's recognition that he must credit God for his current status as one who has been rescued from danger by the forgiveness available only through the sacrifice of Christ. The author's Ebenezer is figurative, but he wants to be reminded that he would have been lost without God's help. I now appreciate the message of this song as being one of the most honest and personal expressions in the hymnal.

In "Come, Thou Fount," Robert Robinson wrote an appreciation for who God is, what he *has* done, and what he *will* do. Robinson begins by acknowledging that no human composition could adequately describe and praise God's true nature, so he asks for a heavenly song to do the job. He then thanks God for the salvation he received personally at the time of his conversion to Christ. Robinson closes the hymn by admitting that he is "prone to leave" the God he loves, and that he is completely dependent on the grace of God to overcome his sinful nature—a vulnerability rarely expressed in most hymns. Robert Robinson's story could belong to any of us—we would do well to raise an Ebenezer to remember what God has done.

PRAYER FOCUS

Spend some time thanking God for how he has worked in you and for the work that he will continue to do.

/// YOUR CUE ///

How has God helped you to the point where you are today?

_____

_____

_____

_____

_____

_____

_____

_____

_____

_____

How frequently do you remember and appreciate what God has done for you?

_____

_____

_____

_____

_____

_____

_____

_____

_____

_____

Do you, like Robert Robinson, sense a powerful tendency to wander away from the God you love? At what times are you likely to do that? What would help you during those times?

_____

_____

_____

_____

_____

_____

_____

_____

_____

_____

I WANT TO BE JUST LIKE YOU

// PERFORMED BY PHILLIPS, CRAIG, & DEAN //

He climbs in my lap for a goodnight hug
He calls me Dad and I call him Bub
With his faded old pillow and a bear named Pooh
He snuggles up close and says, "I want to be like you"
I tuck him in bed and I kiss him goodnight
Trippin' over the toys as I turn out the light
And I whisper a prayer that someday he'll see
He's got a father in God 'cause he's seen Jesus in me

Lord, I want to be just like You
'Cause he wants to be just like me
I want to be a holy example
For his innocent eyes to see
Help me be a living Bible, Lord,
That my little boy can read
I want to be just like You
'Cause he wants to be like me

Got to admit I've got so far to go
Make so many mistakes and I'm sure that You know
Sometimes it seems no matter how hard I try
With all the pressures in life I just can't get it all right
But I'm trying so hard to learn from the best
Being patient and kind, filled with Your tenderness
'Cause I know that he'll learn from the things that he sees
And the Jesus he finds will be the Jesus in me
Right now from where he stands I may seem mighty tall
But it's only 'cause I'm learning from the best Father of them all

/// LIVING WISELY ///

DOUG HARTLEY

a father cannot avoid the fact that he will have a powerful influence on his children. Young eyes will notice whether a father's words match up with his actions. My father was one of those exceptional parents who lived out his faith and didn't just talk about it. I never questioned whether or not my father was sincere in his pursuit to follow Christ. There were many times as a child when I would awake in the middle of the night or in the early morning darkness and notice a light on in the living room. Without my father's knowledge, I would peek around the corner to see him sitting alone, reading his Bible. He wasn't doing this to impress anyone or to teach me a lesson—it was simply a natural expression of who he was. To this day I am inspired by the fact that my dad truly wanted to know God.

Being an example of faith for one's child, or really for anyone who is less advanced in his walk with Christ, cannot be contrived. We can pass on an example of faith only when it flows out of who we truly are. People will learn about Christianity based on our integrity or our hypocrisy, and we should continually remind each other that the stakes are painfully high. If sounding like a Christian is the best we can do, hope of passing our faith on to others is futile. Each of us is imperfect, of course, but we can pray the prayer of this song to be "a living Bible" and "a holy example."

Paul instructed Titus to "encourage the young men to live wisely in all they do. And you yourself must be an example to them by doing good deeds of every kind. Let everything you do reflect the integrity and seriousness of your teaching" (Titus 2:6, 7). This is a tall order, but I am thankful for people like my father who demonstrate that God can help us be consistent role models for those who are watching us. Whether or not you were able to learn from a good example, you can be one to someone else.

PRAYER FOCUS

Pray that God would show you the areas of your life in which you're not living with integrity. Ask God to work in you to make you a living example to those who do not yet know him.

/// YOUR CUE ///

Name some younger people in your life who are watching and learning from you. What have they learned about Jesus from watching you?

_____

_____

_____

_____

_____

_____

_____

_____

_____

_____

_____

If you compromised your integrity in your area of greatest weakness, what would be the consequences for those around you?

_____

_____

_____

_____

_____

_____

_____

_____

_____

_____

Who is a mature Christian in your circle from whom you can still learn? What do you admire in that person?

_____

_____

_____

_____

_____

_____

_____

_____

_____

_____

MAKE A JOYFUL NOISE

// PERFORMED BY DAVID CROWDER //

Make a joyful noise to the Lord
All the earth
Make a joyful noise to the Lord
All the earth

The flowers of the field
Are cry'n to be heard
The trees of the forest
Are singing
And all of the mountains
With one voice
Are joining the chorus of this world

And I will not be silent
I will not be quiet anymore
And I will not be silent
I will not be quiet anymore

Running through the forest
Dive into the lake
Bare feet on beaches white
Standing in the canyon
Painted hills around
The wind against my skin
Every ocean
Every sea
Every river
Every stream
Every mountain
Every tree
Every blade of grass will sing

A DIFFERENT KIND OF PRAISE

DOUG HARTLEY

C ould a blade of grass truly give praise to God? In and of themselves, blades of grass are fairly mundane. The average yard contains thousands of these slender green leaves, and we don't give them much thought. Is it possible that as we walk over a lawn, we are ignoring a vast chorus from the little leafy plants that carpet the ground? In the song "Make a Joyful Noise," David Crowder asserts that, indeed, even grass joins the rest of creation in praising the Lord.

Of course, an individual blade of grass is only a small part of the entire picture of the natural world ascribing greatness to its creator. The psalms are very clear that this concept is true and appropriate. Psalm 148 expresses the idea, instructing: "Praise the LORD from the earth, you great sea creatures and all ocean depths, lightning and hail, snow and clouds, stormy winds that do his bidding, you mountains and all hills, fruit trees and all cedars, wild animals and all cattle, small creatures and flying birds" (Psalm 148:7-10, *NIV*). How can this varied collection of organic and inorganic matter praise God?

It's really quite simple. Everything that God created has a purpose and a special role in the delicate balance of life in the universe. Predators eat, prey is eaten, the winds usher in weather systems, mountains and fields provide a habitat for God's natural drama. All living and nonliving things praise their creator by fulfilling their God-given purposes, with one notable exception: human beings. A kangaroo rat has no choice but to spend its existence doing exactly what God made it to do, but people have a choice. We can decide to worship God with our words and actions, thereby fulfilling our purpose; but we can also choose to pursue godless, indulgent, and destructive lives.

The psalms, along with the lyrics of this song, challenge us to follow the example of nature and acknowledge our reason for existence. We were made to give glory to the one who made us and saved us. All of us have chosen to be silent at one time or another, but we also have the choice to join the chorus of this world and make a joyful noise to the Lord. "I will not be quiet anymore."

PRAYER FOCUS

Ask God to help you see creation through his eyes. Pray that your praise of the creator would be joyful and loud!

/// YOUR CUE ///

Describe a place you have seen that has inspired you to give praise to the creator.

_____

_____

_____

_____

_____

_____

_____

_____

_____

_____

_____

When are you most likely to be distracted from your purpose of worshiping God?

_____

_____

_____

_____

_____

_____

_____

_____

What are some specific reasons you have for appreciating who God is?

_____

_____

_____

_____

_____

_____

_____

_____

What talents or personality traits has God uniquely equipped you with? How can you use these attributes to give God praise?

_____

_____

_____

_____

_____

_____

_____

_____

AMAZING GRACE

// JOHN NEWTON //

Amazing grace! How sweet the sound,
That saved a wretch like me!
I once was lost, but now am found,
Was blind, but now I see.

'Twas grace that taught my heart to fear,
And grace my fears relieved;
How precious did that grace appear,
The hour I first believed.

Thro' many dangers, toils, and snares,
I have already come;
'Tis grace hath bro't me safe thus far,
And grace will lead me home.

The Lord has promised good to me,
His word my hope secures;
He will my shield and portion be,
As long as life endures.

When we've been there ten thousand years,
Bright shining as the sun,
We've no less days to sing God's praise,
Than when we've first begun.

/// THE BEAUTIFUL PARADOX ///

ERIC GOODMAN

amazing grace! The one unforgettable moment in history when the Son of God gave all he was—perfect, pure, and holy—as a living sacrifice for the sake of all men, for all time. This grace is the very essence of hope, the very essence of who we are as Christians.

God has granted direction for the lost and sight for the blind, and all we need is to come before him in full acceptance of his grace. When we truly understand God's mercy and love for us, we can begin to live in that freedom. We no longer have to pretend to be free; our true identity is free.

I can finally acknowledge that I am a fallen child of God. Isn't it great? Here in the moment of humility and acceptance when we grasp what is being offered, we can be witness of a beautiful paradox. "'Twas grace that taught my heart to fear, and grace my fears relieved." We come to realize who we are—the poor in spirit, weak and frail—and we realize all that we have to fear. Yet, joy is abounding. In the very moment we know we ought to die, we realize that we have eternity to truly live.

It is here, in full acceptance, that our lives can authentically reflect the glory of God. Obedience no longer requires an ulterior motive; it becomes a natural outpouring of love on our behalf.

God does not ask us to wallow in our failures or to keep them hidden. It is the direct opposite. He asks us to forget, for he has forgiven. We must stand up, dust off, and let grace be our guide. "'Tis grace hath bro't me safe thus far, and grace will lead me home." "Praise be to the God and Father of our Lord Jesus Christ! In his great mercy he has given us new birth into a living hope . . . and into an inheritance that can never perish, spoil or fade—kept in heaven for you" (1 Peter 1:3, 4, *NIV*). Let this shape who we are; let grace be the very core of how we live and how we worship.

I can't help but love the way this hymn ends—what better ending than the hope of praising God for all eternity!

/// YOUR CUE ///

Have you truly accepted the grace of God?

_____

_____

_____

_____

_____

_____

_____

_____

_____

_____

Have you let him lift the fears and worries from your life? What is one thing that is worrying you? How can you hand that over to God today?

_____

_____

_____

_____

_____

_____

_____

_____

Are you letting go of your failures so that the Spirit of God can take over?

_____

_____

_____

_____

_____

_____

_____

How are you letting God's grace shape your life? How does it daily affect your response to him?

_____

_____

_____

_____

_____

_____

GOD OF WONDERS

// PERFORMED BY CAEDMON'S CALL //

Lord of all creation,
Of water, earth and sky
The heavens are Your tabernacle
Glory to the Lord on high

God of wonders beyond our galaxy
You are holy, holy
The universe declares Your majesty
You are holy, holy
Lord of Heaven and earth
Lord of Heaven and earth

Early in the morning
I will celebrate the light
When I stumble in the darkness
I will call Your name by night

God of wonders beyond our galaxy
You are holy, holy
The universe declares Your majesty
You are holy, holy
Lord of Heaven and earth

Lord of Heaven and earth
Hallelujah to the Lord of Heaven and
    earth
Hallelujah to the Lord of Heaven and
    earth
Hallelujah to the Lord of Heaven and
    earth

God of wonders beyond our galaxy
You are holy, holy
Precious Lord, reveal Yourself to me
Father hold me, hold me
The universe declares Your majesty
You are holy, holy
Hallelujah to the Lord of Heaven and
    earth
Hallelujah to the Lord of Heaven and
    earth
Hallelujah to the Lord of Heaven and
    earth

/// WORLD'S STRONGEST DAD ///

ERIC GOODMAN

When I was very young, maybe five or six years old, I was helping my father clean out our basement. My father handed me all the small things, and I ran them to the appropriate box or threw them in the trash while he was rearranging and taking care of the big-ticket items. After we had been in the basement for a while and made some good headway, we came across my father's old weight set. While it wouldn't seem like much if I found it today, at the time it was a great discovery. My father had all of the weights on one bar—an enormous amount of weight in my eyes. I asked, "Dad, how are you going to move *that*?" but he didn't answer me. Instead, he bent over, grabbed the bar firmly with both hands, and with little effort picked it up past his knees, through his middle section, and above his head. I was in complete amazement at my dad's strength. At that age I had no cognition of the true value of numbers, but I believed that I had just witnessed my father lift what had to be, with the proper conversion, at least be a hundred thousand pounds. No one could possibly be stronger than my dad!

As a child I was easily amazed by things, but I'm no longer so easily impressed. In all honesty I am often guilty of guarding against amazement with skepticism. At what point do we quit allowing ourselves to live in awe and wonder? Why is it so difficult to go before our heavenly Father—the "Lord of all creation, of water, earth and sky"—in an attitude of wonder and amazement? Is it not amazing that we can know the God whose majesty the universe declares? Jesus said, "I assure you, unless you turn from your sins and become as little children, you will never get into the Kingdom of Heaven" (Matthew 18:3).

It pleases God when we humble ourselves like children in awe of their fathers, acknowledging who he is and the power of his glory. Make it a habit to look for the wonder of God in all things. When we worship throughout the day and seek him, we will find him. And the only thing that can follow is wonder—incredible, awesome wonder.

PRAYER FOCUS

I asked my dad, "How are you going to move that?" Isn't it wonderful that we can go before our heavenly Father and know that he can move whatever is in the way? Pray to God, ask him to move whatever it is you need moved. Prepare to be amazed.

/// YOUR CUE ///

In what ways do you connect with God? In what ways are you overwhelmed with the wonder of who he is?

_____

_____

_____

_____

_____

_____

_____

_____

_____

_____

_____

Do you find him most easily through prayer, music, nature, or relationships with others? How can you create more opportunities to connect with God in this way?

_____

_____

_____

_____

_____

_____

_____

_____

_____

_____

_____

Take time every day this week to seek God in the way you named and reflect on how it changes the way you feel about worshiping him.

_____

_____

_____

_____

_____

_____

_____

_____

_____

_____

OUR GREAT GOD

// **PERFORMED BY THIRD DAY** //

Eternal God, unchanging, mysterious and unknown
Your boundless love unfailing, in grace and mercy shown
Bright seraphim in endless flight around your glorious throne
They raise their voices day and night in praise to you alone
Hallelujah! Glory be to our great God!
Hallelujah! Glory be to our great God!

Lord, we are weak and frail, helpless in the storm
Surround us with your angels; hold us in your arms
Our cold and ruthless enemy, his pleasure is our harm.
Rise up, O Lord, and he will flee before our Sovereign God
Hallelujah! Glory be to our great God!
Hallelujah! Glory be to our great God!

Let every creature in the sea and every flying bird;
Let every mountain, every field and valley of the earth;
Let all the moons and all the stars in all the universe
Sing praises to the living God, who rules them by his word
Hallelujah! Glory be to our great God!
Hallelujah! Glory be to our great God!

/IMPLY THE GREATE/T

ERIC GOODMAN

ry to imagine what it means be eternal, to have infinite duration—it is just beyond our comprehension. We live in a dynamic world— things are constantly changing and very few things endure. Because we are in the world, we are pulled to change. Our emotions are in flux and we are inconsistent. We lack continuity in our choices between right and wrong, in our motivation that fluctuates between being selfless and egocentric, and in whether we follow our hearts or our minds. And that is far from being an exhaustive list.

Sadly our constancy with God is similarly challenged. One week my devotion to God is increasing steadily, and three weeks later I fail to recall the last time I spent quality time with God. Or maybe I'm on my way to church, already experiencing the presence of God and anticipating powerful worship, but I let intense traffic stress me out and remove my focus from where it *should* be. God does not always get my best—or our best. This is our struggle.

We have all been inconsistent and fallen short of God's eternal glory. "We are weak and frail, helpless in the storm." Thankfully our ability to move in his direction is not dependent on us—it's only possible through his eternal goodness. We must know that there is a power greater than any we can fathom, any the world can create. When our ruthless enemy throws temptation at us, we must call on the power of God and watch the devil flee. "In his kindness God called you to his eternal glory by means of Jesus Christ. After you have suffered a little while, he will restore, support, and strengthen you, and he will place you on a firm foundation" (1 Peter 5:10). It's such a relief to be able to cry out and sing, "Hallelujah! Glory be to our great God!" He whose character never compromises is eternally offering himself and his unfailing love to us.

How can this not be the greatest thing that life has to offer? We are invited into a relationship with the creator of the world. He is the God who rules every creature, every mountain, every field, every valley, and every star in the universe by his living Word.

When we strip ourselves of pride, hand over our lives, and recognize the greatness of the one true God, there is freedom. And in this freedom we can recognize more and more of the glory of God. Let us worship God for all the things we are not—the characteristics that make him great and that give us strength to run hard after him. "Praise him for his acts of power; praise him for his surpassing greatness" (Psalm 150:2, *NIV*).

PRAYER FOCUS

Take time to focus on God's surpassing greatness. The glory of God is all around us and is waiting to be praised. Pray about how his glory might be seen through you, for we were meant for his glory.

/// YOUR CUE ///

Do you believe that God is the only thing you cannot go without?

_____

_____

_____

_____

_____

_____

_____

_____

_____

_____

_____

Are there things in your life that hinder you from seeing the greatness of God?

_____

_____

_____

_____

_____

_____

_____

_____

_____

_____

_____

How can you show God in your daily worship that you understand and accept that you need to lean on his strength and goodness?

_____

_____

_____

_____

_____

_____

_____

_____

_____

_____

_____

HALLELUJAH
(YOUR LOVE IS AMAZING)

// BRENTON BROWN & BRIAN DOERKSEN //

Your love is amazing,
steady and unchanging
Your love is a mountain,
firm beneath my feet
Your love is a mystery,
how you gently lift me
When I am surrounded,
your love carries me

Hallelujah, Hallelujah
Hallelujah, your love makes me sing
Hallelujah, Hallelujah
Hallelujah, your love makes me sing

Your love is surprising,
I can feel it rising
All the joy that's growing
deep inside of me
Every time I see you,
all your goodness shines through
And I can feel this God song,
rising up in me

/// WITNESS OF LOVE ///

MARCELLA FARMER

music means so much to almost everyone I know. Even the least musical person I know likes to listen to the radio and owns a number of CDs. And those friends who will not sing when they think people might hear them will sing when they're alone in their cars. Many of us are drawn to express ourselves through singing. It makes sense that this worship song focuses on our natural tendency to sing. We cannot help but sing to express the joy that we experience because of the love that God has for us.

It's always interesting to participate in corporate worship services and see how different people worship. If you've been in front of a congregation during a worship service, you might have noticed that some people in the congregation do not express joy. They often stand with their arms crossed, looking as if they have no intention of worshiping God . . . ever. When I am up front helping to lead in worship, I always hope that my eyes will not land on one of those people—the reasons may be obvious. People who do not express joy in worship do not encourage me in my worship, and it's very easy to be distracted by them and assume that they're not experiencing God's love in a meaningful way. The people who lift me up the most during a worship service are the ones who are not afraid to lift their voices to God—regardless of how off-key they might be. These people are not singing to impress anyone. They know the love of God and want to praise him because of it.

In Acts 16 we read about Paul and Silas who, after having been severely beaten, were imprisoned. While in prison, these men sang praises to God. Paul and Silas knew that God loved each of them even as he was allowing them to suffer for his sake. And they testified to that love while the other prisoners listened. In the midst of an apparent trial, God's love sustained Paul and Silas, and God used them to bring an entire household to know him.

Regardless of our circumstances—whether we're in a worship service, alone in the car, or being treated unjustly—we can worship God in song and experience the joy that comes through doing so. Hallelujah, God's love *is* amazing!

PRAYER FOCUS

Pray that you would give your whole heart to God in worship. Ask God to guard you from distractions that threaten to take your focus away from him. Ask that he help you find meaningful worship in every circumstance, and that he would accept your worship as a gift.

/// YOUR CUE ///

Can you think of examples of how God's love is all of the things that are described in this worship song?

_____
_____
_____
_____
_____
_____
_____
_____
_____
_____
_____

Are you afraid to be heard singing praises to God, or are you trying to impress others when you sing in worship?

_____
_____
_____
_____
_____
_____
_____
_____
_____
_____

Pray that God will help you to be authentic in worship.

_____
_____
_____
_____
_____
_____
_____
_____
_____
_____

LOVE SONG FOR A SAVIOR

// PERFORMED BY JARS OF CLAY //

In open fields of wildflowers,
She breathes the air and flies away
She thanks her Jesus for the daisies and
the roses
In no simple language
Someday she'll understand the meaning
of it all

He's more than the laughter or the stars
in the heavens
As close as a heartbeat or a song on her
lips
Someday she'll trust Him and learn how
to see Him
Someday He'll call her and she will
come running
And fall in His arms and the tears will
fall down and she'll pray,

"I want to fall in love with You"
"I want to fall in love with You"
"I want to fall in love with You"
"I want to fall in love with You"

Sitting silent wearing Sunday best
The sermon echoes through the walls
A great salvation through it calls to the
people
Who stare into nowhere, and can't feel
the chains on their souls

It seems too easy to call you "Savior,"
Not close enough to call you "God"
So as I sit and think of words I can
mention
To show my devotion

"I want to fall in love with You"
"I want to fall in love with You"
"I want to fall in love with You"
"My heart beats for You"

/// PERFECT LOVE ///

MARCELLA FARMER

a love song for anyone other than that special man or woman in your life may seem rather strange. Love songs usually express romantic feelings and all the gushy, sweet stuff that makes some of us want to be sick. So why write a love song to the Savior? It may seem inappropriate to view our relationship with Jesus in a romantic way, but think about it—in a way, our relationship with Jesus really is romantic. The Savior chose to leave the riches of his kingdom to come to earth and live as a man to save the ones he loves. Love stories don't get any more intense than the sacrificing of one person's life for another. And the sacrifice that Jesus made is much more valuable than a sacrifice that any person on earth can make for one he loves. The perfect love of Jesus allows us the opportunity to experience an eternal love and life with the Father. So why are so many people hesitant to accept the perfect love of God through Jesus?

Some say that they have difficulty understanding how a father can be good because of the bad experiences they have had with their earthly fathers. I like to think of God as the ideal Father who knows how to be so much more than the father that I have on earth. Even those who do know the good love of a human father are aware that sometimes their fathers make mistakes. However, God never makes mistakes, and that is something in which we can trust.

Others say they cannot receive God's love until they clean up their lives. Romans 5:8 says, "God proves his love for us in that while we still were sinners Christ died for us" *(NRSV)*. One of the most passionate aspects of the love that Jesus has for us is that we do not have to impress him or try to win his love. His love meets us where we are, but it does not expect us to stay there.

According to Jesus, the greatest command is to love God with all your being. When we truly realize the depth of the Savior's love for us, we cannot help but fall in love with him.

/// YOUR CUE ///

Is there something keeping you from knowing and accepting the fullness of the sacrifice Jesus made for you?

_____

_____

_____

_____

_____

_____

_____

_____

_____

_____

_____

Do you live as one who has been saved by love?

_____
_____
_____
_____
_____
_____
_____
_____
_____
_____

What are some ways in which you can show your devotion to God?

_____
_____
_____
_____
_____
_____
_____
_____
_____
_____

NOTHING TO SAY

// PERFORMED BY ANDREW PETERSON //

Hey, Jamie, would you mind
Driving down this road awhile
Arizona's waiting on these eyes
Rich is on the radio
And I think we ought to take it slow
Arizona's caught me by surprise

Hey, Jamie, have you heard
"A picture paints a thousand words"
But the photographs don't tell it all
I see the eagle swim the canyon sea
Creation yawns in front of me
O Lord, I never felt so small

And I don't believe
That I believed in You
As deeply as today
I reckon what I'm saying is
There's nothing more
Nothing more to say

And the mountains sing Your glory
   hallelujah
The canyons echo sweet amazing grace
My spirit sails
The mighty gales are bellowing Your
name
And I've got nothing to say
No, I've got nothing to say

Hey, Jamie, do you see
I'm broken by this majesty
So much glory in so little time
So turn off the radio
Let's listen to the songs we know
All praise to Him who reigns on high

Hey, Jamie, would you mind
Driving down this road awhile
Arizona's caught me by surprise

/// CAN YOU SEE HIM? ///

MARCELLA FARMER

ndrew's song reminds me of a favorite day from my past when I was studying at a small college in northeastern Tennessee. I had to stay on campus during fall break because of a non-school commitment, and not very many other students were around. Thankfully, a couple of my good friends were among the few who had stayed in town. The three of us decided to use some of our spare time to take a day trip. Our destination was about two hours away in North Carolina. It was such a beautiful fall day, and the drive was magnificent as we surveyed the varying colors of leaves on the trees. We spent hours walking trails and being awed by the splendor and creativity of our creator. Although it was not the Grand Canyon, I think I have tasted what Andrew is describing in this song.

Our God is so big and capable of so much that we just cannot begin to comprehend. Maybe you haven't visited the Grand Canyon or the mountains of North Carolina. What was your response when you first visited some other great wonder? Most likely, you were silent for a while as you gazed in amazement at the handiwork of God. Perhaps you thought about how small you are in comparison. You might relate to David's words in Psalm 8:3, 4: "When I look at your heavens, the work of your fingers, the moon and the stars that you have established; what are human beings that you are mindful of them, mortals that you care for them?" *(NRSV).* You can step outside and see the awesomeness of God in any part of nature. Just look at the vastness of the sky or even the intricacies of a spider web. When you take time to observe God's creation, you cannot help but be overwhelmed.

We need to live in awe of the creator. In Psalm 46:10, God says, "Be silent, and know that I am God!" When we have time with God, we can be so focused on asking for things that we do not take enough time just to be in the presence of God and experience the wonder of who he is. Will you join with the mountains in singing his praise?

PRAYER FOCUS

Ask God to help you be more aware of his power and the effect that it can have on your life.

/// YOUR CUE ///

Look around you right now. In what people or things can you see God's creativity right where you are?

_____

_____

_____

_____

_____

_____

_____

_____

_____

_____

_____

Are you silent before God on a regular basis, taking in the magnificence of who he is?

_____

_____

_____

_____

_____

_____

_____

_____

_____

What small change can you make in your life to help you stop being so focused on yourself and to become more focused on God?

_____

_____

_____

_____

_____

_____

_____

_____

_____

_____

REST IN YOU

// PERFORMED BY WATERDEEP //

All of my fears and trials, Lord, all of my
  doubts, all of my shouts
All of my fears and trials, Lord, rest in
  You
All that I love and hold, O Lord, all of my
  songs, all of my longings
All that I hold and love, O Lord, rest in
  You

You're loving, You're patient, You're
  strong and true
All goodness, all mercy are found In You
All of the praises of the earth rest in You

All of our fears and trials, Lord, all of our
  doubts, all of our shouts
All of our fears and trials, Lord, rest in
  You
All that we love and hold, O Lord, all of
  our songs, all of our longings,
All that we hold and love, O Lord, rest
  in you

You're loving, You're patient, You're
  strong and true
All goodness, all mercy are found in You
All of the praises of the earth rest in You

All praise to the one who loves me
All praise to the one who cares

All of our worries and our shame
All of our hiding, all of our fighting
All of our worries and our shame rest in
  You

All of our greatest victories, Lord, all of
  our passions all that we have
Everything we hold back, O Lord
We rest in You.

All praise to the one who loves me
All praise to the one who cares

All praise to the one who loves me
All praise to the one who cares
Oh, how He cares.

All of the praises of the earth, they rest
  in You.
All of the praises of the earth, rest in
  You.
All of the praises of the earth, rest in
  You.

/// THE RHYTHM OF REST ///

MELISSA SANDEL

how often do you rest? The concept of resting was introduced into the world at the time of creation. God created the world; and Scripture tells us that "by the seventh day God had finished the work he had been doing; so on the seventh day he rested from all his work" (Genesis 2:2, *NIV*).

Even the God of the universe understood the value of rest and set that standard for us. Yet in our busy, twenty-first-century culture, the desire to work, produce, and accomplish can consume our lives. Many people rise in the morning asking, "How much can I get done today?" We rush across town from event to event. Working long hours, running errands, spending time with others, functioning from commitment to commitment, the lives of most Americans are consumed with the stresses of life. Not only are our bodies busy, but our minds are busy as well. We worry about the future, we face trials, and we think about the burdens of life.

We have longings and concerns that keep our minds busy even when our bodies try to rest. But when God is at the center of our lives and at the core of our livelihood, we have the ability to rest in him. What does this really mean? All of our fears and trials can subside because he will carry them for us. God desperately wants his children to experience the refreshment that comes with rest. He knows everything about us and understands the deep complexities of life, everything we love, and everything we long for. When we make a concentrated effort to depend on our creator, we can rest all of these things in him. He loves us and cares for us. Because of his passion for his people, he wants us to release our worries, our shame, and our busy schedules into his hands. God desires for us to be refreshed and ready for the journey.

Pray that God will give you times of rest and peace in the coming week. Ask God to show you the things that you need to eliminate from your life because they keep you too busy to rest in his presence. Pray that you will continue to know God more deeply and, in so doing, understand his provision and care more fully.

/// YOUR CUE ///

Rest is vital to our survival. Rest from work, as well as rest from our thoughts, is needed in order to continue living a Spirit-filled life. How long has it been since you have let your body and your mind rest? God has created you for the *re*-creation that occurs in resting. Will you rest in him?

_____

_____

_____

_____

_____

_____

_____

_____

Read Genesis 1 and 2. Why did God rest on the seventh day? Why does the author of Genesis include this information?

_____

_____

_____

_____

_____

_____

_____

_____

_____

_____

_____

_____

When is the last time you were well rested? What keeps you from resting in the Lord?

_____

_____

_____

_____

_____

_____

_____

_____

What does your typical day look like? Are there things that need to be eliminated in order for you to live a Spirit-filled life?

_____

_____

_____

_____

_____

_____

_____

_____

_____

SHIFTING SAND

Sometimes I believe all the lies
So I can do the things I should despise
And every day I am swayed
By whatever is on my mind

I hear it all depends on my faith
So I'm feeling precarious
The only problem I have with these
  mysteries
Is they're so mysterious

And like a consumer I've been thinking
If I could just get a bit more
More than my 15 minutes of faith,
Then I'd be secure

My faith is like shifting sand
Changed by every wave
My faith is like shifting sand
So I stand on grace

I've begged you for some proof
For my Thomas eyes to see
A slithering staff, a leprous hand
And lions resting lazily

A glimpse of your back-side glory
And this soaked altar going ablaze
But you know I've seen so much
I explained it away

Waters rose as my doubts reigned
My sand-castle faith, it slipped away
Found myself standing on your grace
It'd been there all the time

My faith is like shifting sand
Changed by every wave
My faith is like shifting sand
So I'll stand on grace . . .
Stand on grace . . .

/// *TAP, TAP, TAP, JUMP!* ///

MELISSA SANDEL

It was a special game shared between her and her father. When her mother was away, her daddy would put her tiny, four-year-old feet on top of the long kitchen counter, which was set up as an island in the middle of the kitchen. He would stand at the end of the counter, as was their tradition. "Here I come, Daddy!" she would exclaim. And without thinking twice, her big curls would begin to bounce. *Tap, Tap, Tap, Tap, Tap,* Jump! With her hands extended, she would jump headfirst into her father's arms, and he would catch her as she flew off the counter. The little girl played this game repeatedly, giggling and cuddling in her father's arms as he caught her fall. Of course, this was a game that could be played only when Mommy wasn't home, for mothers rarely enjoy seeing their four-year-old daughters flying in midair.

One night before bed, the little girl's mother needed something from the store. It was a stormy night, and her mother would be gone only for a few minutes. Rushing to get her pajamas on, the little girl knew that this would be a prime opportunity to play the special game. In her little footy pajamas, she was placed on top of the counter. But as her father took his position at the end of the counter, the sound of thunder filled the house. "Here I come, Daddy!" Just as she took her first step, the house went black and the electricity went out. *Tap, Tap, Tap, Tap, Tap,* Jump! Without hesitation and without the ability to see the arms that would catch her, she jumped headfirst into her father's arms. And as always, his arms wrapped around her, catching and holding her as they giggled together in the dark.

We need to trust our Father much like the little girl trusted her daddy. Jesus challenges his followers to abandon everything and follow him with faith like a child—the pure, trusting, recklessly abandoned faith of a young child. Yet living life with a childlike faith is so much more difficult than it sounds. So many things keep us from looking out into the darkness and jumping headfirst with a faith that trusts that our Father will catch us.

Like consumers, we frequently want just a little more faith before we're willing to jump. At other times we just need more proof. *God, I will jump into your will and into your arms if you will simply prove yourself to me one more time.* We forget that throughout history and throughout our lives, God has proven his faithfulness time and time again.

While God's faithfulness is unwavering, our "faith is like shifting sand changed by every wave." Thank God for grace! It is, in fact, God's grace that gives us the security to take a leap of faith, trusting that our Father will catch us. What step of faith is God calling you to take? What excuses are you using that keep you from jumping into his will? Will you humble yourself with the faith of a child? "Here I come, Daddy!" *Tap, Tap, Tap, Tap, Tap,* JUMP!

PRAYER FOCUS

Pray that God will reveal to you the next steps that you need to take in your faith. Pray that he will help you identify barriers in your spiritual life and that he will help you remove them. Pray for the courage and strength needed to recklessly abandon your own hesitation for the arms of God.

/// YOUR CUE ///

What proof has God given you in the past year that reaffirms his faithfulness? his power? his grace? In the past month? In the past week?

_____

_____

_____

_____
_____
_____
_____
_____

Read Matthew 14:22-32. Why do you think Peter got out of the boat? What kept the others from doing the same?

_____
_____
_____
_____
_____
_____

What circumstances are causing you to stay in the boat? What are the deeper issues in your life that cause you to doubt?

_____
_____
_____
_____
_____
_____
_____

What step of faith might God be calling you to take?

_____
_____
_____
_____

THERE IS A REDEEMER

// PERFORMED BY KEITH GREEN //

There is a redeemer,
Jesus, God's own son,
Precious lamb of God, Messiah,
Holy one,

Jesus my redeemer,
Name above all names,
Precious lamb of God, Messiah,
Oh, for sinners slain.
Thank you, O my Father,
For giving us your son,
And leaving your spirit,
'Til the work on earth is done.

When I stand in glory,
I will see his face,
And there I'll serve my king forever,
In that holy place.
Thank you, O my Father,
For giving us your son,
And leaving your spirit,
'Til the work on earth is done.

There is a redeemer,
Jesus, God's own son,
Precious lamb of God, Messiah,
Holy one,
Thank you, O my Father,
For giving us your son,
And leaving your spirit,
'Til the work on earth is done.
And leaving your spirit,
'Til the work on earth is done.

/// COMPLEX SIMPLICITY ///

MELISSA SANDEL

There is a Redeemer. *Redeem* simply means "to exchange for something of value." Jesus exchanged his life for a beautiful prize of great value—your life. There is a Redeemer. He is Jesus, God's own Son. He is the precious Lamb of God. He is the Messiah. He is the holy one. He did *nothing* wrong. He was perfect.

We, on the other hand, are far from perfect. God gives us two commands: love God and love people. But somehow, following these two commands seems too difficult. We make poor choices and blame others. We experience pain and frequently blame God. We do what we want to do, when we want to do it, rather than live the life that God has called us to live. We prefer comfort to obedience. We are prideful. We get angry. We become selfish. We are sinful. We deserve nothing. Yet while we were still sinners, Jesus the Redeemer died for us. He exchanged his life for our lives. And this is the gospel story.

We make the gospel story complex. Granted, it is mysterious. And it is radical. But it was never meant to be complex. The most mysterious and radical thing about the story of Jesus is that it is so simple. Sometimes we forget the beauty of its simplicity. Jesus is in the business of redeeming people. He loves to buy back the lost, the weary, and the sinful. He offers us the chance to trade our meaningless lives for something of value—lives filled with the Holy Spirit and the promise of amazing life to come for all of eternity. This is the simple gospel story.

Because our stories intersect the gospel story, we are loved for exactly who we are—no strings attached. Because our stories intersect the gospel story, we are able to overcome our struggles. No challenge is too big. Because our stories intersect the gospel story, we have the power to be who we want to be, and we have the power to do amazing things in God's name. We can change the world. And all of this is possible because there is a Redeemer who exchanged his life so that we might live.

And the gospel story doesn't just stop with the redemption of individuals. God left his Holy Spirit here until his redeeming business is completed here on earth. This means that not only is there a Redeemer but also there is a loving, authentic, and redeeming community here on earth that is possible through the work of Holy Spirit—the church.

PRAYER FOCUS

Thank our Father for giving us his Son and leaving his Spirit here to dwell within us. Ask God to help us understand the simplicity of what it means to be redeemed and to be a part of helping others experience redemption.

/// YOUR CUE ///

Who was the first person to explain the gospel to you? Take a few minutes to pray, thanking God for that person.

_____

_____

_____

_____

_____

What is the most difficult thing for you to understand about redemption?

_____

_____

_____

_____

_____

_____
_____
_____
_____
_____
_____
_____
_____

What can you do this week to show God's redemption to other people (your family members, friends, coworkers) in a practical way?

_____
_____
_____
_____
_____
_____
_____
_____
_____

What does a redeeming community look like? How can you help your church become a redeeming community?

_____
_____
_____
_____
_____
_____
_____
_____
_____
_____

ALL THE WAY MY SAVIOR LEADS ME

// PERFORMED BY RICH MULLINS //

All the way my Savior leads me
What have I to ask beside?
Can I doubt His tender mercy,
Who through life has been my Guide?
Heav'nly peace, divinest comfort,
Here by faith in Him to dwell!
For I know, whate'er befall me,
Jesus doeth all things well;
For I know, whate'er befall me,
Jesus doeth all things well.

All the way my Savior leads me
Cheers each winding path I tread,
Gives me grace for every trial,
Feeds me with the living Bread.
Though my weary steps may falter
And my soul athirst may be,
Gushing from the Rock before me,
Lo! A spring of joy I see;
Gushing from the Rock before me,
Lo! A spring of joy I see.

All the way my Savior leads me
O the fullness of His love!
Perfect rest to me is promised
In my Father's house above.
When my spirit, clothed immortal,
Wings its flight to realms of day
This my song through endless ages:
Jesus led me all the way;
This my song through endless ages:
Jesus led me all the way.

Words by Fanny J Crosby. Public Domain.

/// THE GOOD ∫HEPHERD ///

hroughout the Bible, God often led people to new places without telling them exactly where or why they were going. Whether he was leading a desert nomad named Abram to a new home, bringing a few million Hebrew slaves out of Egyptian captivity behind a pillar of flame, or sending a scandalous young couple to Bethlehem for a census, God guided and protected his people. This care and leadership is the basis for the common metaphor of God as the shepherd of his people.

While the idea that God is our shepherd can be comforting, the idea that we are a bunch of smelly sheep is not nearly so pleasant. Anyone who has worked with sheep knows that they are quite possibly the dumbest four-legged animals in all creation. They stand out in the rain, they'll overeat until they're sick, and if left to their own devices, they're liable to wander off a cliff. This is all too often an accurate, if not particularly complimentary, reflection of the way people behave when they try to live without a Savior, a good shepherd to lead them.

But perhaps the one saving quality of sheep is that they are willing to follow someone they can trust—a shepherd. Jesus describes himself as the good shepherd, one who can lead his sheep by the sound of his voice. Like any good shepherd, he provides for all aspects of his flock's well-being. He nourishes and refreshes his charges with his own body as the bread of life (John 6:32-58). He disciplines *and* shows mercy to the obstinate and disobedient; he comforts the hurting; he gives rest to the weary. When a sheep loses its way, Jesus seeks to rescue it regardless of the danger or cost to himself. He protects his flock from thieves and marauders who seek to steal and destroy them. He laid down his own life to keep the sheep from being forever lost.

Christ's sacrifice on the cross enabled him to lead us on the final leg of the journey prepared for us. By his death and resurrection, the way to eternal rest with the Father in Heaven is open to all who will follow him. Thus our Savior truly does lead us all the way, even beyond this life.

PRAYER FOCUS

Thank God for his protection and ask for his guidance in your life.

/// YOUR CUE ///

How does the biblical view of people as sheep compare with the world's views of human reason and self-sufficiency?

_____

_____

_____

_____

_____

_____

_____

_____

_____

_____

In what ways has Christ protected you from those who seek to steal and destroy? How has his guidance protected you from yourself?

_____

_____

_____

_____

_____

_____

_____

_____

Read Psalm 23:1-4. What does David mean when he writes "your rod and your staff protect and comfort me"?

_____

_____

_____

_____

_____

_____

_____

_____

_____

_____

THE ANCHOR HOLDS

// PERFORMED BY RAY BOLTZ //

I have journeyed
Through the long dark night
Out on the open sea
By faith alone
Sight unknown
And yet His eyes were watching me

The anchor holds
Though the ship is battered
The anchor holds
Though the sails are torn
I have fallen on my knees
As I faced the raging seas
The anchor holds
In spite of the storm

I've had visions
I've had dreams
I've even held them in my hand
But I never knew
They would slip right through
Like they were only grains of sand

I have been young
But I am older now
And there has been beauty these eyes have seen
But it was in the night
Through the storms of my life
Oh, that's where God proved
His love to me

/// ANCHOR OF FAITH ///

PHIL MANN

We have this hope as an anchor for the soul, firm and secure" (Hebrews 6:19, *NIV*).

Life ain't easy, and the Christian life is certainly no exception. While some people naively believe that being a Christian will shelter them from any earthly troubles, Ray Boltz reminds us in "The Anchor Holds" that Christians experience storms in life just like anyone else. The difference is the effect these events have on a believer's life. While most of us won't face the literal storms that threatened Jesus and his disciples (Luke 8:24) or Paul (Acts 27), we all will face turmoil and troubles throughout our time on earth. When these troubles seem about to capsize us, we can rely on God's promised blessings as a source of strength.

The storms we experience can be great opportunities for God to display his power to his people and the world. Jesus didn't rebuke the storm in Luke 8:24 until the disciples were in fear for their lives. This demonstration of God's power over nature amazed the same men who had seen Jesus heal the sick, raise the dead, and forgive sins! These storms can also be a test of faith. Throughout the history of Israel, God used invasions and enslavement by neighboring peoples to remind the Israelites of the true source of their strength.

Whatever the reason for the trials in life, God promises that he will not abandon his people to face them alone. Though Jesus prophesied that his followers will face persecution until the end times (Luke 21:12-19), he also promised to provide the words and wisdom to respond to persecutors, and that though we may be put to death, in the end we will gain life. Regardless of the intensity of the circumstances we're facing, God will meet our needs. Though we may face great temptation, God will always provide a way out of the situation (1 Corinthians 10:13).

One of the most powerful examples of God's faithfulness is his promise to Abraham to make his descendants a great nation. Abraham held onto God's promise as God led him to a new home in a distant land, protected him from the locals (and his own mistakes), and finally enabled his wife to bear him a son. We can take hope in the fact that God fulfills his promises to us just as he did for Abraham! This hope can serve as an anchor for the soul in even the worst storms of life.

PRAYER FOCUS

Thank God for his faithfulness in times of trouble. Lift up to him any crises in your life that you feel you're facing alone.

/// YOUR CUE ///

Think of a recent "storm" you have experienced (or are currently experiencing). How has your faith in God's promises kept you anchored? Where might you have drifted without this hope?

_____

_____

_____

_____

_____

_____

_____

_____

_____

_____

_____

Are you able to recognize God's power during "storms" in your life? Is it easier to see after life has calmed down?

_____

_____

_____

_____

_____

_____

_____

_____

_____

_____

Does it seem easy to drift away from God during smoother times in your life?

_____

_____

_____

_____

_____

_____

_____

_____

_____

_____

I DO BELIEVE

// PERFORMED BY STEVEN CURTIS CHAPMAN //

Sitting in a traffic jam 11:52 p.m.
Just a few miles south of Cincinnati, Ohio
I take my pen and start to write
The thoughts that fill my head tonight
Nothing terribly profound
Just these simple words
That keep my heart anchored down
That keep my restless heart anchored down

I do, I do, I do, I do believe
I know, I know, I know, I know it's true, yeah
I do, I do, I do, I do believe
Lord, I believe in You
I believe in You

Now these can be confusing times
The skeptics posing as the wise
It's hard to see the light
Through all the shadow of the doubt
But You keep saying all the while
It takes the vision of a child
Looking through the eyes of faith to see reality
So once again I will say
I believe You're the life
You're the truth, You're the way

If this faith in You is blind
It's not to anything that's true
'Cause Your love opens up my eyes
To see that everything I need
Is found when I believe in You, yeah

/// FAITH STEPS ///

"Is there really a God?" "Does he really love me?" "Did Jesus rise from the dead?" "Is this stuff really true?"

I've wrestled long and hard with doubt over the last decade of my life. At times I felt as if I were being swallowed up by hopelessness and drowning in a sea of uncertainty. As a result of facing doubt, I made a lot of assumptions. I assumed that all those doubtful thoughts were mine, and if they were mine, then there must be something wrong with me. I felt as if I was the only one who struggled with doubt and that I wasn't like "true" believers who never doubt. Doubt fed on doubt and challenged my own salvation!

What I failed to realize was that my assumptions could be way off. I didn't appreciate that in order for doubt to exist, faith also must exist and even precede doubt. I failed to realize that doubt may be a smoke screen for any number of problems. It could be that Satan is lying to me and trying to strip me of my faith, or that my emotions are all out of whack. There may be some unresolved issue nagging at me unconsciously, some sin pulling my attention to it rather than to God. I might have a wrong understanding of God or faulty expectations about life. When doubts hit, I failed to exercise the faith God had given me, and I chose to feed the doubt.

After a friend of mine suffered a debilitating illness, I had a more clear understanding of the importance of exercising faith. My friend was confined to a wheelchair while she was recovering, but even after her body had been healed, she still couldn't walk. There was nothing seriously wrong with her body; the problem was just that her muscles were too weak to enable her to stand. Her muscles needed to be exercised in order to gain the strength to walk again. Faith must also be exercised in order to grow and be strengthened.

When we face circumstances that require us to stand on our legs and make a step of faith, we allow God to be God and to reveal himself to us. God isn't bent out of shape when we doubt, and he is powerful enough to validate himself when we let him. But doubt can be dealt with only by making a step of faith. If it is truly our desire to know God, we can get there only by personally experiencing him, and we can experience him only when we surrender to him and take the first step on faith. After each step our faith grows and our doubts subside. God works in our lives to show us who he really is. Not only does God show himself, he also resolves those issues in our lives that caused doubt in the first place. When we begin to walk by faith and face our doubt, God becomes clearer and more beautiful than ever.

"I do believe, but help me not to doubt!" (Mark 9:24).

PRAYER FOCUS

Ask God to strengthen your muscles of faith by encouraging you to step out in faith. Ask and anticipate that you will experience his walking beside you when you do take those steps.

/// YOUR CUE ///

Has there ever been a time when you didn't live by faith? What was the outcome? What effect did it have?

_____

_____

_____

_____

_____

_____

Has there ever been a time when you *did* live by faith? What was the outcome? What effect did it have?

_____

_____

_____

_____

_____

_____

_____

_____

_____

In what areas of your life is God asking you to walk in faith now? And if you are hesitating, why?

_____

_____

_____

_____

_____

_____

_____

_____

_____

IF YOU WANT ME TO

// PERFORMED BY GINNY OWENS //

The pathway is broken
And the signs are unclear
And I don't know the reason why you
brought me here
But just because you love me the way
that you do
I'm gonna walk through the valley
If you want me to

'Cause I'm not who I was
When I took my first step
And I'm clinging to the promise you're
not through with me yet
So if all of these trials bring me closer
to you
Then I will go through the fire
If you want me to

It may not be the way I would have
chosen
When you lead me through a world that's
not my home
But you never said it would be easy
You only said I'll never go alone

So when the whole world turns against
me
And I'm all by myself
And I can't hear you answer my cries for
help
I'll remember the suffering your love put
you through
And I will go through the darkness
If you want me to

'Cause when I cross over Jordan
Gonna sing, gonna shout,
Gonna look into your eyes and see you
never let me down
So take me on the pathway that leads
me home to you
And I will walk though the valley
If you want me to

Yes, I will walk through the valley
If you want me to

Words by Ginny Owens and Kyle Matthews. © 1999
Rocketown Records, LLC., BMG Songs, Inc. (Gospel
Division)/Above the Rim Music (Administered by BMG Songs,
Inc.). All rights reserved. Used by permission.

/// REFINING FIRE ///

PHIL VAN MILLIGAN

I used to view suffering as a sign that I had somehow lost favor with God; but as I surrendered to him and embraced the trials laid before me, I began to see those challenges in an entirely different light. Now when I go through the valleys, I see the changes that occur in me: I see my character enhancing, my understanding increasing, and my love growing. I become more like Jesus, who also embraced suffering. And I can rest in the knowledge that God loves me enough to go through all the effort of walking me through the valleys of life in order to refine my character and make me more like Jesus.

I now have the perspective that the valleys of life are not strokes of bad luck or punishment from a judgmental God, but the opportunities of change given to us by a loving Father. They are opportunities to learn more about him and his unending love for us. More than that, they are an encouragement in that the Lord of the universe deems us worthy and believes that we can handle his refining work. It's also encouraging that he understands how it feels to go through hardships because he went through the valleys himself.

My sinful nature always wants to take the path of least resistance in order to avoid pain at all costs. My new nature understands that the Father's way is more often the harder way, and it requires submission and a step of faith. But it's in that process that we gain greater intimacy with God and a peace beyond understanding. When we have made it through the valley, our praise to him is deeper and all the more sweet.

When the next valley lies before us, we can approach it with greater faith instead of fear. We can say with a new attitude, "This is going to be hard, but I'm thankful that I won't go through it alone, and I look forward to what God is going to do as a result of it."

My best times are not those when everything is problem-free and life is easy, but those times following hardship and pain. It's in those times that I can look back and say, "God is good! Look what he brought me through! Look how he's changed me!" It's in those times that I feel God's love because I've experienced his loving me enough to change me, to purify me, and to test me.

PRAYER FOCUS

Thank God for the work he is doing through times of pain and suffering. Reflect on times past in which God's work was accomplished through hard times, and trust him with the hard times you are currently going through. Anticipate that he is and will accomplish good through them.

/// YOUR CUE ///

How has God shown you his power and love through your suffering?

_____

_____

_____

_____

_____

_____

_____

_____

_____

_____

Do you see hardship as a punishment or as an opportunity? Do you hold a grudge against God during suffering, or do you submit to his will?

_____

_____

_____

_____

_____

_____

_____

_____

_____

_____

Do you typically pray during hard times for God to get you out of the valley, or do you ask him to use the valley as he sees fit to teach, test, or change you?

_____

_____

_____

_____

_____

_____

_____

_____

_____

_____

WELCOME HOME

// PERFORMED BY SHAUN GROVES //

Take me, make me
All You want me to be
That's all I'm asking, all I'm asking
Welcome to this heart of mine
I've buried under prideful vines
Grown to hide the mess I've made.

Inside of me,
Come decorate, Lord
Open up the creaking door
And walk upon the dusty floor
Scrape away the guilty stains
Until no sin or shame remains
Spread Your love upon the walls
And occupy the empty halls
Until the man I am has faded
No more doors are barricaded

Come inside this heart of mine
It's not my own
Make it home
Come and take this heart and make it
All Your own
Welcome home

Take a seat, pull up a chair
Forgive me for the disrepair
And the souvenirs from floor to ceiling
Gathered on my search for meaning
Every closet's filled with clutter
Messes yet to be discovered
I'm overwhelmed, I understand
I can't make this place all that You can

I took the space that You placed in me
Redecorated in shades of greed
And I made sure every door stayed
locked
Every window blocked, and still You
  knocked

Take me, make me
All You want me to be
That's all I'm asking, all I'm asking

/// PLACE OF SURRENDER ///

PHIL VAN MILLIGAN

take me, make me all You want me to be. That's all I'm asking, all I'm asking." Is this your heart's cry? Living out that statement requires complete surrender on our part, and it's impossible to find the fullness of life that Jesus offers until we reach this point of complete submission.

Surrender is one of the hardest things to achieve because it hits at the core problem in our selfish, sinful nature. We want to do things our way, we want to do things that make us feel good, we want to have things that makes our lives easier, we want to look good, be popular, have power, be important, be self sufficient. . . . But when we decide to indulge our selfishness, we begin to pull away from real loving relationships with others, God, and ourselves. We have all, just like Eve and Adam, decided to do things our way rather than God's way and have ended up hiding in the bushes. Too ashamed to show our faces and too proud to show our sins, we decide to sit there. But because of God's amazing love for us, he comes looking for us; and he doesn't stop until he finds us in the midst of our sin and shame.

It is at this place—where we feel the most worthless and unlovable—that the God of all creation fully loves us and says we are worth dying for. God sees us as we really are, loves us unconditionally, and is dying for one thing: for us to surrender to him by saying, "'Welcome to this heart of mine I've buried under prideful vines, grown to hide the mess I've made. Inside of me, come decorate' and make it *your* home."

When we get to the point where we give him our hearts, Jesus pulls up a chair and talks with us as a friend. He begins a remodeling process inside us. He redecorates and cleans out all the garbage that we've allowed to build up. He transforms us from the inside out. When we surrender ourselves to God, we surrender our sins, our shame, our control, our masks we hide behind, our desires to be perfect or better than we are, and our pride. In the place of the people we have allowed ourselves to become, God comes in and gives us new identities and begins to make us the people *he* wants us to be—the people he created us to be, the people that we truly are. And that's the beauty of surrender.

PRAYER FOCUS

Pray for God to search your heart and reveal any area he would like to enter and change. Submit your life to God so that he can reflect his transforming power through you from the inside out.

/// YOUR CUE ///

What is your heart's cry? Is it for God to make you all that he wants you to be?

_____

_____

_____

_____

_____

_____

_____

_____

_____

_____

How have you seen transformation in your life that reflects God's remodeling work inside you? Are their rooms in your heart that you need to let God renovate? What is God asking you to surrender next?

_____

_____

_____

_____

_____

_____

_____

_____

_____

_____

Do you find yourself hiding behind masks in front of others, or are you being true to the person God made you to be?

_____

_____

_____

_____

_____

_____

_____

_____

_____

_____

BIG ENOUGH

// PERFORMED BY CHRIS RICE //

None of us knows and this makes it a mystery
If life is a comedy, then why all the tragedy?
Three-and-a-half pounds of brain try to figure out
What this world is all about
And is there an eternity, is there an eternity?

God, if You're there I wish You'd show me
And, God, if You care then I need You to know me
I hope You don't mind me asking for Your cue
But I figure You're big enough
I figure You're big enough

Lying on pillows we're haunted and half-awake
Does anyone hear us pray, "If I die before I wake?"
Then the morning comes and the mirror's another place
Where we wrestle face-to-face with the image of deity
The image of deity

When I imagine the size of the universe
And I wonder what's out past the edges
Then I discover inside me a space as big
And believe that I'm meant to be
Filled up with more than just Your cue

So, God, if You're there I wish You'd show me
And, God, if You care then I need You to know me
I hope You don't mind me asking for Your cue
But I figure You're big enough
I figure You're big enough
'Cause I am not big enough

/// A STEP OF FAITH ///

SARAH EICHENBERGER

I think it's relatively easy to understand why those who are not Christians question God, the reality of God, and the existence of Heaven. They refuse to step out in faith because they want to *know* all of the answers before coming to Christ. But what if, horror of horrors, we Christians have those same doubts and unanswered questions?

Actually, I think that the yearning for truth impacts Christians even more strongly than it does non-Christians. I feel that for those who pursue God intensely, the pain of not knowing it all hits us more sharply. It's the same pain that made Lucifer fall from Heaven, the same pain that caused Adam and Eve to falter in the Garden—the desire for the knowledge that only God possesses. Because without it, how will we *really* ever know?

How do we *know* that a whole lifetime of following Jesus will really result in an indescribable eternity? Why, if I am doing everything I am supposed to be doing, am I not happy? Why do I still endure intense suffering?

When God gave Solomon the opportunity to have the one thing that he desired, Solomon chose wisdom. Over riches, or women, or happiness, he chose wisdom. And even with that wisdom, he cried out in Ecclesiastes over the paradoxes of the world—wickedness being favored on this earth over righteousness, and why bad things happen to good people. It seems that the more he knew, the more questions resulted. I think the same is true for us.

It all seems to come down to one question: do we believe that God is truth? Solomon closes his sermon in Ecclesiastes with this statement: "Here is my final conclusion: Fear God and obey his commands, for this is the duty of every person." (Ecclesiastes 12:13) After all of his lamenting of how meaningless this life is and his wrestling with what it all adds up to, his answer was simply to fear God and follow his instructions. Even if there is only one belief that we can hang onto, that God is truth, let us trust in Jesus and let him take care of the rest. Because even though we don't have all of the answers to the questions we're going to struggle with, God is "big enough" to handle each one.

PRAYER FOCUS

Pray that you would hold tight to the belief that God is truth. Ask that God would use you to help someone else take a step of faith.

/// YOUR CUE ///

How does Solomon's advice impact you? Does it encourage you or leave you feeling tired?

_____

_____

_____

_____

_____

_____

_____

_____

_____

_____

What is the biggest doubt that you're facing right now?

_____
_____
_____
_____
_____
_____
_____
_____
_____
_____
_____

HARD TO GET

// PERFORMED BY RICH MULLINS //

You who live in heaven
Hear the prayers of those of us who live
    on earth
Who are afraid of being left by those we
    love
And who get hardened by the hurt

Do you remember when You lived down
    here where we all scrape
To find the faith to ask for daily bread
Did You forget about us after You had
    flown away
Well I memorized every word You said
Still I'm so scared I'm holding my breath
While You're up there just playing hard
    to get

You who live in radiance
Hear the prayers of those of us who live
    in skin
We have a love that's not as patient as
    Yours was
Still we do love now and then

Did You ever know loneliness
Did You ever know need
Do You remember just how long a night
    can get
When You were barely holding on
And Your friends fall asleep
And don't see the blood that's running in
    Your sweat
Will those who mourn be left
    uncomforted
While You're up there just playing hard
    to get

And I know you bore our sorrows
And I know you feel our pain
And I know it would not hurt any less
Even if it could be explained
And I know that I am only lashing out
At the One who loves me most
And after I figured this somehow
All I really need to know

Is if You who live in eternity
Hear the prayers of those of us who live
    in time
We can't see what's ahead
And we cannot get free of what we've left
    behind
I'm reeling from these voices that keep
    screaming in my ears
All the words of shame and doubt blame
    and regret
I can't see how You're leading me unless
    You've led me here
Where I'm lost enough to let myself be
    led
And so You've been here all along I
    guess
It's just Your ways and You are just plain
    hard to get

/// CHAƧING GOD ///

SARAH EICHENBERGER

this is one of my favorite songs by Rich. In it, he so beautifully illustrates the struggle between head and heart when it comes to our relationship with Christ. Rich holds nothing back as he unabashedly questions God about his presence and his empathy for his children.

Rich uses the image of "playing hard to get," an image most often assigned to thoughts of dating relationships. The very presence of this analogy is the product of our minds' trying to grasp what is ultimately an infinite idea of God and bring it down to our level—trying to package God up so that we can feel more comfortable with the depth of him, making him pocket-size and easier to handle.

As I was thinking about how to write this devotional, I kept wondering, *There are so many questions that this song brings up, but no answers. How am I supposed to answer these questions?!* I was tortured with this responsibility. I sought out advice, searched the Bible for answers, but everything just led to more mystery. Then I realized, more clearly than I ever could have without this process, that this is what this song is about. We try so hard to figure God out—what his plans are, how he works—that sometimes we miss him actually doing his work right in front of our faces. We miss his plan unfolding before us. I was worrying so much about how to write this devotional that I missed God's point. He was calling me to question what I believed about him and to realize that I don't have all the answers either.

God isn't easy to take in. He's not easy to understand. The more we try to bring him down to size, the more he will seem elusive and incomprehensible. I can't tell you why God does the things he does. I can't tell you what his plan is for each of us. But I can tell you that he does have a plan—a complicated, intricate, beautifully written plan. When you get to the place where you are questioning all of these things, it might just be exactly where he's led you to be.

/// YOUR CUE ///

Hindsight is 20/20. Can you look back on your life and see how God has led you according to his plan, while you were none the wiser?

_____

_____

_____

_____

_____

_____

_____

_____

_____

_____

_____

Do you ever feel frustrated with God? his timing? his plan?

_____

_____

_____

_____

_____

_____

_____

_____

_____

_____

IF I STAND

There's more that rises in the morning
Than the sun
And more that shines in the night
Than just the moon
It's more than just this fire here
That keeps me warm
In a shelter that is larger
Than this room

And there's a loyalty that's deeper
Than mere sentiments
And a music higher than the songs
That I can sing
The stuff of Earth competes
For the allegiance
I owe only to the Giver
Of all good things

So if I stand let me stand on the
    promise
That you will pull me through
And if I can't, let me fall on the grace
That first brought me to You
And if I sing let me sing for the joy
That has born in me these songs
And if I weep let it be as a man
Who is longing for his home

There's more that dances on the prairies
Than the wind
More that pulses in the ocean
Than the tide
There's a love that is fiercer
Than the love between friends
More gentle than a mother's
When her baby's at her side

And there's a loyalty that's deeper
Than mere sentiments
And a music higher than the songs
That I can sing
The stuff of Earth competes
For the allegiance
I owe only to the Giver
Of all good things

CREDIT WHERE CREDIT IS DUE

SARAH EICHENBERGER

We need to be losers. Before you close the book and decide that you now hate the book AND the song, hear me out. I'm sure you have a lot in your life to be proud of. Some of us take pride in our career accomplishments, some in our love for our families, some in being a great Christian. But I'm going to challenge you to call yourself a loser and forget anything that you are proud of.

OK, seriously, don't close the book.

Pride is the most dangerous thing in our lives, and the reason is simple: it puts blinders on us that make us see only things of this world, things that our feeble minds can fathom, things our weak hands can accomplish. Our life can become a kind of résumé that we ramble off to people in order to look intelligent or impressive.

Look around you. Look at all of the things that you have done, all of the amazing things around you, the intelligence of the technology that mankind has developed, the goodness that we bestow upon one another. Now realize that those things are only a fraction of what exists beyond what we can see or do or even imagine. Nothing we make or accomplish can ever compare to what God can do. He has merely blessed us with gifts that we can certainly enjoy in our time on earth. But these gifts are only a small sliver of all that he is.

When you look at what God has done, the love he has for us, and the beautiful and intricate creation that he has lavished us with, our seventh-grade track meet medals look a little silly, don't they?

So be a loser! Realize that anything we can do is only because God has given us that gift or ability. That panhandler whom you made smile by giving him your extra pizza? That was God working through you! That presentation you weren't prepared for but somehow pulled off with the expertise of a seasoned pro? That was God's wisdom graciously lent to you. The patience you demonstrated when your child decided to make scarves out of your favorite sweater? Yep! God again!

We are losers without God, so stop trying to impress and start taking pride in the God who made you so impressive!

PRAYER FOCUS

God has given you gifts perfectly made for you. Thank him for these and pray for the humility to use them for his glory, not your own, and for the wisdom to discern the difference.

/// YOUR CUE ///

What are your top three accomplishments?

_____

_____

_____

_____

_____

_____

_____

_____

_____

_____

_____

What are your top five favorite qualities about yourself?

_____

_____

_____

_____

_____

_____

_____

_____

_____

_____

Can you look at your lists and see how God is behind each
accomplishment and quality?

_____

_____

_____

_____

_____

_____

_____

_____

_____

_____

LOVER

// PERFORMED BY DEREK WEBB //

Like a man comes to an altar,
I came into this town,
With the world upon My shoulders
And promises passed down.
When I went into the water,
My Father, He was pleased.
I built it and I'll tear it down
So you will be set free.

Yes, and I found thieves and salesmen
Living in My Father's house.
And I know how they got in here,
And I know how to get 'em out.
Well, I'm turning this place over
From floor to balcony.
Then, just like these doves and sheep
Oh, you will be set free.

'Cause I have always been a lover
From before I drew a breath
Oh, and some things I love easy
And some I love to death.
You see, love's no politician
'Cause it listens carefully
So from those who come,
I can't lose one,
So you will be set free,
Oh, you will be set free.

Go on and take My picture
Go on and make Me up
Oh, I'll still be your Defender
And you'll be My missing son
And I'll send out an army
Just to bring you back to Me.
'Cause regardless of your brothers' lies,
Oh, you will be set free.

Because I am My beloved's
And My beloved's Mine;
So, you bring all your history,
I'll bring the bread and wine.
Then we'll have us a party
Where all the drinks are on Me
And as surely as the rising sun
Oh, you will be set free,
Oh, you will be set free.

/// A LOVE LIKE NO OTHER ///

SARAH EICHENBERGER

ove. One of the most often pondered, over-analyzed, and rarely understood things in the world. Most of the greatest secular songs ever written were written about love—understanding what it is, what it takes, what it gives. They speak of losing love, breakups, and heartaches—things we all have surely experienced in our relationships along the way. For example, I'm sure you have heard one of these statements at one point or another:

"I just don't love you anymore."
"I can't forgive you."
"It's not you; it's me."

Human love fails. We will always fail each other because we are not capable of the kind of love God has for us. But we *are* capable of receiving that kind of love. The hard part is believing that that love exists and, more importantly, that it is ours for the taking.

I came from a Christian family, grew up in the church, and studied the Bible daily at a Christian school. But later in life I strayed from the church and the Christian lifestyle in an attempt to flee the binding rules and seek freedom by living for myself. When that life crumbled beneath me, I had nothing to break my fall. *God doesn't love me,* I thought. *Maybe he did before when I was living for him, but he could never love someone like me, not after all that I've done.* That's when a friend played the song "Lover" for me, and it forever changed my life and my understanding of how much God loves *me,* his sinful servant.

It's easy to think often of the righteous and just God that we are so familiar with in the Old Testament. The omnipotence of the God we serve is too powerful to ignore and yet almost too mighty to embrace. It is so tempting to think that when we screw up, God's love for us is weakened or may even disappear. Blame it on fire and brimstone sermons if you will, a lot of us focus a bit too much on God the punisher. We often forget God the lover who weeps for us when we choose to break through the boundaries he put into place to protect us. We equate his love with the human love that fails us, but his love doesn't go away when we turn our backs on him. It stays constant, waiting for us to accept it. In other words, it's not him; it's YOU!

PRAYER FOCUS

Learning to accept God's love will surely be a lesson you will learn over and over again in your lifetime. Pray that God will break down whatever barriers you have put up between you and his unfailing love.

/// YOUR CUE ///

Think about a time when you had your heart broken. What were the human reasons that relationship failed?

_____

_____

_____

_____

_____

_____

_____

_____

_____

_____

_____

Do you believe that God loves you unconditionally?

_____

_____

_____

_____

_____

_____

_____

_____

_____

_____

THIƧ WORLD

// PERFORMED BY CAEDMON'S CALL //

There's tarnish on the golden rule
And I wanna jump from this ship of fools
Show me a place where hope is young
And a people who are not afraid to love

This world has nothing for me and this world has everything
All that I could want and nothing that I need

This world is making me drunk on the spirit of fear
So when you say who will go, I am nowhere near

'Cuz this world has nothing for me and this world has everything
All that I could want and nothing that I need

But the least of these look like criminals to me
So I leave Christ on the street

This world has held my hand and has led me into intolerance
So now I'm breaking up, now I'm waking up
I'm making up for lost time

This world has nothing for me and this world has everything
All that I could want and nothing that I need
This world has nothing for me and this world has everything
All that I could want and nothing that I need

THINGS ARE NOT AS THEY SEEM

SARAH EICHENBERGER

// Dedicated to the life of Schroeder Berg //

here is a lie that is constantly being sold to us. We go to church, we read our Bibles, we learn right from wrong. Then we leave the church building, go to our places of work, visit our friends, watch our televisions—and we see a completely different vision of how we should live. We ask ourselves, *Is* this *what people my age are supposed to be like? Is* that *what I should be doing?*

The world offers everything you could ever want. As the song says, "This world has held my hand." It gently courts you with the pleasures and acceptance that your heart desires. It is so easy to slip into musing that maybe the world is right and you are wrong. Maybe there is something to this world in front of us, something we've missed out on by always doing the "right thing" and trying to follow God.

God confronted those musings by allowing me to contemplate some real shortcomings of this world. I suffered the misfortune of two acquaintances dying this past summer—one a Christian, the other not. From the outside, I observed the differences in the grieving processes of two families when faced with this very real and ultimate question of life.

The non-Christian's memorial service was one of complete anguish. It was the human condition at its absolute lowest point. Looking at the faces of friends and family, I saw no trace of the knowledge of life that Christ offers. Their faces reflected their complete dissolution of hope and their overwhelming sense of finality.

My Christian friend died just as suddenly and just as tragically—at the peak of his faith and walk with Christ. To some it seemed an inexplicable loss. At the young man's funeral, friends and loved ones mourned his broken body and his life cut short. Yet, in the midst of the service, the boy's mother was dancing and waving her arms in the air, rejoicing for her son's new life in Heaven!

Things are not as they appear in this world! Jesus has given us a privileged view into the somewhat paradoxical differences between what we see and what he sees. He gives us the knowledge that there is more to this world than what we can see—and he has so much more waiting for us.

PRAYER FOCUS

It can be hard to believe sometimes. Pray that you will always know that God is truth. Pray for the guidance to know the difference between the truth and the lie and for the courage to always choose the truth.

/// YOUR CUE ///

Is anything in this world tempting you to discredit God?

_____

_____

_____

_____

_____

_____

_____

_____

_____

_____

What is one instance you can recall that God used to show you that there is more to life than this world has to offer?

_____

_____

_____

_____

_____

_____

_____

_____

_____

_____

_____

ALL CREATURES OF OUR GOD AND KING

// PERFORMED BY DAVID CROWDER //

All creatures of our God and King,
Lift up your voice and with us sing,
O praise Him! Alleluia!
Thou burning sun with golden beam,
Thou silver moon with softer gleam!
O praise Him, O praise Him!
Alleluia! Alleluia! Alleluia!

Thou rushing wind that art so strong,
Ye clouds that sail in heav'n along,
O praise Him! Alleluia!
Thou rising morn, in praise rejoice,
Ye lights of evening, find a voice!
O praise Him, O praise Him!
Alleluia! Alleluia! Alleluia!

And all ye men of tender heart,
Forgiving others, take your part,
O sing ye! Alleluia!
Ye who long pain and sorrow bear,
Praise God and on Him cast your care!
O praise Him, O praise Him!
Alleluia! Alleluia! Alleluia!

Let all things their Creator bless,
And worship Him in humbleness,
O praise Him! Alleluia!
Praise, praise the Father, praise the Son,
And praise the Spirit, Three in One!
O praise Him, O praise Him!
Alleluia! Alleluia! Alleluia!

Words by St. Francis of Assisi. Public Domain.

/// LIGHTNING CRASHES ///

STEPHEN JONES

have you ever been stuck outside on a hot, stale day? Even standing still in the shade brings you to a sweat. Before you can find your next air-conditioned retreat, the sky begins to darken and the clouds roll across the horizon. In a flash a cool forceful wind kicks up and pins the shirt against your back. You are overwhelmed by the smell of rain. It seems as if, in a matter of moments, a symphony of feeling and relief has been composed around you.

Minutes later, the earth soaked and tossed, dark clouds begin to break. Illuminated from behind, they hint at a marvelous revelation to come. A ray of sunshine breaks through, touching the puddles now reflecting like mirrors. The sun you once cursed now illuminates a painting in the sky. Red, orange, and purple usurp the space which gray and black occupied. Large, thick storm clouds are replaced by rolling canvases of pink. Your eyes stare in amazement.

God is *huge*. He is *everywhere*. He is in *everything*. This is his creation. His canvas. His symphony. It was made by his hand and reflects his glory. God is such a part of our surroundings that they cannot help but offer him praise. Consequently it doesn't make much sense to look at a sunset and wonder who decided on the color. Or listen to water run down a creek and ask why it makes such a peaceful sound while it flows over the rocks. The frozen ground cannot contain God's glory—it bursts forth with new life each spring. God's beauty cannot be masked by the barren trees of winter—mounds of white decorate them as the snow falls.

1 Chronicles 16:31, 32 proclaims: "Let the heavens rejoice, let the earth be glad; let them say among the nations, 'The LORD reigns!' Let the sea resound, and all that is in it; let the fields be jubilant, and everything in them!" *(NIV).* Driving down a highway early one summer, I witnessed the type of jubilant fields to which that verse

refers. Wildflower seeds had been spread in the median and on the sides of the freeway. The rough asphalt, pounded daily by hundreds of automobiles, weaved through an overgrown field of poppies and baby's breath. Even so, the gravel and weeds could not suppress the beauty of the creation that was calling out his name. "O praise Him! Alleluia!"

PRAYER FOCUS

Pray to the God who made you. With the same craftsmanship he used to create the sunset, he created you. Ask God to make his greatness evident in your life.

/// YOUR CUE ///

Where have you experienced God's creations bringing glory to his name?

_____

_____

_____

_____

_____

_____

_____

_____

_____

How does God expose his greatness to you? What can you do to become more aware of it?

_____

_____

_____

_____
_____
_____
_____
_____
_____
_____
_____

What can you do to become more in tune with your creator?

_____
_____
_____
_____
_____
_____
_____
_____

How can you match your every step with God's praise?

_____
_____
_____
_____
_____
_____
_____

WHATEVER THING

// PERFORMED BY WATERDEEP & 100 PORTRAITS //

Whatever thing
that I have carried in this place
that will keep me from you
I will lay it at your feet
Whatever burden
I have carried for so long
that will keep me from seeing you
I will lay it down right now

I need to hear you speak to me
I want to feel you in this place
You long to take me in your arms of love
So take me in your arms of love

All of the things
that are cluttering my mind
I will push them far from here
and listen for your voice
All of the pain
that I am carrying inside
I will hand it to you
and you will take it
Set me free
And I will fly

I need to hear you speak to me
I want to feel you in this place
You long to take me in your arms of love
So take me in your arms of love
So take me in your arms of love

/// ʃHHH . . . ///

STEPHEN JONES

he more baggage and burdens we carry, the more easily we are prevented from being fully available to the Lord's direction and presence. Our minds' being occupied with distractions stands in the way of our hearts' being completely open. When our hearts are troubled and hardened, our minds struggle to get past the pain—that makes it difficult to focus on Christ and to know that he is near. But at the same time, Jesus doesn't treat us with indifference when we're battling to overcome distraction.

I don't believe that God waits to speak to us until those times when we are properly prepared and focused on him. Our Lord just chooses to speak to us where we are so that we don't have to stay in that place. His desire to have a personal relationship with us is overwhelming. His yearning never wavers. And he longs for our worship.

When we come to worship, God wants to reveal himself to us as we praise him. But when we don't stop to listen or be open to the Holy Spirit's moving, we miss that revelation. This is when a feeling of distance surfaces. It's easy to blame God for this. "God is just far away from me right now." "I just don't know where God fits in." During times like these, faith begins to lose some of its relevance. Doubts and questions ring out louder as the barrier between me and the one who made me grows. It becomes difficult to focus at all. I begin to question my ministry and its effectiveness. Eventually all that remains is the question "Is God real?"

Feeling far from God is an all-too-common experience for me—so much so that I have a designated place to go in times like these. I have found my refuge near a mountain with a small lake, and I take my burdens and questions there. But after a day or so, it's just a mountain and a lake. In places like that, God shows me that he never swayed. It becomes obvious that his love and power are steadfast. He never turned his back on me. He did not stop trying to show himself. His Holy Spirit was always there, waiting for me to surrender my burdens, clear my head, and begin listening.

In all actuality there is no magical place where God can be heard over the clutter. Our ability to commune with God has much more to do with the state of our hearts than with the quiet or chaos of our surroundings. God speaks and can be heard if our prayers are like that of King David's: "Create in me a clean heart, O God. Renew a right spirit within me. Do not banish me from your presence, and don't take your Holy Spirit from me. Restore to me again the joy of your salvation, and make me willing to obey you" (Psalm 51:10-12).

PRAYER FOCUS

Pray that you will be able to put aside any baggage you're holding onto. Pray that you will be fully available to God's direction and praise.

/// YOUR CUE ///

How do you prepare for worship? Do you use Bible reading? a CD? quiet?

_____

_____

_____

_____

_____

_____

_____

_____

_____

What are some of the things that clutter your mind? How can those be eliminated?

_____

_____

_____

_____

_____

_____

_____

_____

_____

_____

_____

How can you make yourself available to hear God's voice in the midst of your busy life?

_____

_____

_____

_____

_____

_____

_____

_____

_____

_____

_____

BE THOU MY VISION

// PERFORMED BY DAVID CROWDER //

Be Thou my vision
O Lord of my heart
Naught be all else to me
Save that Thou art
Thou my best thought
By day or by night
Waking or sleeping
Thy presence my light

Be Thou my wisdom
And Thou my true word
I ever with Thee and
Thou with me, Lord
Thou my great Father and
I Thy true son
Thou in me dwelling
And I with Thee one

Riches I heed not
Nor man's empty praise
Thou my inheritance
Now and always
Thou and Thou only
First in my heart
High King of heaven
My treasure Thou art

High King of heaven
My victory won
May I reach heaven's joys
O bright heavens' sun
Heart of my own heart
Whatever befall
Still be my vision
O Ruler of all

Words by Mary E. Byrne and Eleanor Hull. Public Domain.

/// ULTIMATE JOY ///

STEVE DAMON

I t is no simple thing to make Christ the "High King" of our hearts. Despite the fact that the relationship Christ offers is more precious than gold, more satisfying than the richest of foods, more delightful than the intimacy of lovers, we constantly turn toward ephemeral, sinful pleasures and forsake his kindness. As fallen creatures we must struggle against sin and press on toward contentment in Christ. We must strive to keep Christ first in our hearts so that we are more taken up with him than with any earthly things.

The best earthly gifts are mere *shadows* of God's greatness, and we have the freedom to enjoy them either to the glory of his name or to the destruction of our souls. When we choose to satiate ourselves with inferior, sinful pleasures, the satisfaction we experience is fleeting and earthbound. Conversely the deepest joy and contentment available to any of us come from knowing God and having a deep and meaningful relationship with him.

This relationship is experienced when we invite God to dwell in our hearts. And after the victory is won, we will be taken up with the pleasure of glorious relationship with our creator in Heaven. Our finite minds will be dazzled with visions of his infinite greatness. We will always desire more of him *and* constantly be satisfied in him. As our understanding of his depth and brilliance and glory intensifies, we will delight to worship the "High King" of Heaven for eternity.

/// YOUR CUE ///

What earthly pleasures distract you from finding joy in Christ?

_____

_____

_____

_____

_____

_____

_____

_____

_____

_____

_____

Read 1 Corinthians 10:31. In view of Heaven, how should we enjoy the pleasures that God has given us on earth?

_____

_____

_____

_____

_____

_____

_____

_____

_____

_____

Read Matthew 25:1-13. How should a heavenly minded Christian live on earth?

_____

_____

_____

_____

_____

_____

_____

_____

_____

_____

IN CHRIST ALONE

// **KEITH GETTY & STUART TOWNEND** //

In Christ alone my hope is found
He is my light, my strength, my song
This cornerstone, this solid ground
Firm through the fiercest drought and
storm
What heights of love, what depths of
peace
When fears are stilled, when strivings
cease
My comforter, my all in all
Here in the love of Christ I stand

In Christ alone, who took on flesh
Fullness of God in helpless Babe!
This gift of love and righteousness
Scorned by the ones He came to save
'Til on the cross as Jesus died
The wrath of God was satisfied
For every sin on Him was laid
Here in the death of Christ I live

There in the ground His body lay
Light of the world by darkness slain
Then bursting forth in glorious day
Up from the grave He rose again!
And as He stands in victory
Sin's curse has lost its grip on me
For I am His and He is mine
Bought with the precious blood of Christ

No guilt in life, no fear in death
This is the power of Christ in me
From life's first cry to final breath
Jesus commands my destiny
No power of hell, no scheme of man
Can ever pluck me from His hand
'Til He returns or calls me home
Here in the power of Christ I'll stand

/// FOREVER PERFECT ///

STEVE DAMON

What aspect of our salvation in Christ do you find most amazing? Certainly God's ways are above our ways and worthy of our worship! He reigns in perfect holiness and cannot possibly overlook even the slightest sin that we commit. We deserve to experience his wrath in Hell forever. Yet he has made a way for us to have with him a more intimate relationship than we can have with any other person in the universe.

Christ is the "gift of love and righteousness" that has satisfied God's wrath so that we might live. Jesus came into the world and walked among men, knowing full well that he would be hated. Yet he chose to die at the hands of the self-righteous, to make it possible for those very men to be saved and live in Heaven with him. And while Satan gleefully celebrated every minute of the beating, flogging, and crucifixion of Jesus, his evil plan was actually the sovereign Lord's perfect plan to destroy evil forever. What glory is due his name!

There is no god like our God. In Christ alone we find hope. In him alone is the power to free us from the curse of sin. We live in the death of Christ because the wages of sin is death and the gift of God is eternal life in Christ Jesus. From all nations Christ, the bridegroom, is gathering the church, his bride, to delight in him in Heaven forever! So be glad, for there is no greater power in which we can stand every day, no greater reward for which we can persevere, than Christ alone!

PRAYER FOCUS

Spend some time thanking God for loving you so much that he sent a perfect sacrifice so that you might spend eternity with him. Ask God to give you the strength to stand in Christ.

/// YOUR CUE ///

Read Romans 8:1-4. What has the power of Christ done for us that we could never achieve on our own?

_____

_____

_____

_____

_____

_____

_____

_____

_____

_____

_____

Read John 17:1-5. What is the chief goal of God in carrying out his plan of salvation?

_____

_____

_____

_____

_____

_____

_____

_____

_____

_____

What aspect of our salvation in Christ do you find most amazing?

_____

_____

_____

_____

_____

_____

_____

_____

_____

_____

WE ARE HUNGRY

// PERFORMED BY STEVE FEE //

Lord, I want more of You
Living water rain down on me
Lord, I need more of You
Living breath of life come fill me up

We are hungry, we are hungry
We are hungry for more of You
We are thirsty, O Jesus
We are thirsty for more of You

Lord, I want more of You
Holy Spirit rain down on me
Lord, I need more of You
Living breath of life come fill me up

We lift our holy hands up
We want to touch You
We lift our voices higher
And higher and higher to You

/// LIVING BREATH OF LIFE ///

STEVE DAMON

Wanting more of Christ is not just an idea to sing about during corporate worship. It should affect every aspect of our lives. To want more of Christ is to want less of worldly distractions. It means less TV, less surfing the Web, and less stuff. To want more of Christ is to yield your selfish desires to his godly commands. It means less angry yelling, less grudge-holding, less getting your way. If you want more of Christ, you can have more by reading his Word, serving your neighbor, forgiving a loved one who has hurt you, and rejecting opportunities for sin. Then when you cry out to the one who made you, you will feel the "living breath of life" filling you up.

It is always God's will for us to want more of Christ. And even if we don't feel this desire, God will give it to us if we ask. But we need a healthy perspective on what having more of Christ is. When we sing these words, we should not be thinking, *I want a more emotional experience during worship.* We should be thinking, *I want to be so taken up with the supremacy of Christ and his God-glorifying, soul-saving work that my affections are driven to worship him above all else!*

After we awaken to the inadequacy of enjoying creation while ignoring the creator, we are compelled to want to know more of Christ. When we experience the emptiness of our souls without him, we feel a hunger to know him more. As we detect the shallow nature of sinful pleasures, our living water (the Holy Spirit who lives in believers) stirs our hearts. We repent of our wandering desires and seek to occupy our minds with his greatness.

PRAYER FOCUS

Pray that God would cause your heart to desire him more than
worldly pleasures. Ask that he would help you find your greatest
satisfaction in him.

/// YOUR CUE ///

Is wanting more of Christ truly at the root of your enjoyment of
worshiping him?

_____

_____

_____

_____

_____

_____

_____

_____

_____

_____

_____

Read Philippians 3:7-16. How did Paul express his desire to want more of Christ?

_____

_____

_____

_____

_____

_____

_____

_____

_____

_____

Read 1 Peter 2:2, 3 and Hebrews 5:11-14. Do you need "spiritual milk" or "solid food" to satisfy your hunger for Christ?

_____

_____

_____

_____

_____

_____

_____

_____

_____

_____

GOD IS IN CONTROL

// PERFORMED BY TWILA PARIS //

This is no time for fear
This is a time for faith and determination
Don't lose the vision here
Carried away by emotion
Hold on to all that you hide in your heart
There is one thing that has always been true
It holds the world together
God is in control
We believe that His children will not be forsaken

God is in control
We will choose to remember and never be shaken
There is no power above or beside Him, we know
God is in control

History marches on
There is a bottom line drawn across the ages
Culture can make its plan
Oh, but the line never changes
No matter how the deception may fly
There is one thing that has always been true
It will be true forever

He has never let you down
Why start to worry now?
He is still the Lord of all we see
And He is still the loving Father
Watching over you and me

/// BLINDED BY FEAR ///

TABITHA NEUENSCHWANDER

Fear. Carried away by emotion. Both describe what my every thought and action were ruled by. I thought it was the norm to always second-guess myself. It made for a stressful life, but I figured that's the way things were supposed to be for everyone.

Last fall my fear and emotions began to affect me in such a way that I became physically ill. I would become light-headed, cry randomly, and even faint. After several visits to a doctor and a visit to a psychologist, I was diagnosed with clinical depression.

My life wasn't going the way I had planned. I was living in a city I wanted nothing to do with—in my parents' basement. At work I was moved from a position I loved to a position I *strongly* disliked. And my personal relationships weren't exactly going the way I wanted. Everything in my life was about me, and the more I tried to control my world, the more it fell apart. I was sure that God wasn't talking to me when he said, "For I know the plans I have for you. . . . They are plans for good and not for disaster, to give you a future and a hope" (Jeremiah 29:11). I had lost all vision of why God would want to use me.

As I began to work through my junk, God showed me otherwise. He has helped me work through past hurts and trials. It's been a painful and frustrating journey. There have been times when I wanted to give up, but there was something inside me that knew God was going to use my dark times for good. And so I managed to hold on.

It's been almost a year since my world came crashing in on me. It has been with much prayer and support from friends and family that I've made it this far. It's amazing how much good has come out of my darkness. I am still in the same city, but it's OK—God wants me here. I'm about to move out of my parents' house and begin a new adventure. I have moved to a cool new position at work, and my relationships are stronger than they were a year ago.

I live in amazement of how much freedom I have gained by giving God control of my life.

PRAYER FOCUS

Ask God to show you what specific area of your life he wants you to release. Ask God to show you how to let go and give control to him.

/// YOUR CUE ///

What do you need to let God have control of?

_____
_____
_____
_____
_____
_____
_____
_____
_____
_____
_____

Why are you afraid to let him have control?

_____

_____

_____

_____

_____

_____

_____

_____

_____

_____

Name at least one person who can keep you accountable in giving
control to God.

_____

_____

_____

_____

_____

_____

_____

_____

_____

_____

LOVER OF MY SOUL

// PERFORMED BY AMY GRANT //

When I see the Winter turning into Spring
Oh, it speaks to this heart of mine
More than anything
Underneath a blanket of snow, cold and white
Something is stirring in the still of the night

And then the sun comes up, slowly with the dawn
Oh, this is the kind of feeling
That I hang my hope upon
There is love and beauty in all that I see
And no one, nobody, is explaining You to me

Maybe my eyes can't see
But You are surrounding me
Here in the wind and rain
The things that I know
Tender and sweet, and strong as my need
I know the voice, I know the touch
Lover of my soul

And when the evening comes, and sunlight fades to red
And time and time and time again
I whisper in my head
"Give me strength, give me faith," to fully believe
That the Maker of this whole, wide world
Is a Father to me

/// ʃEEIПG GOD ///

TABITHA NEUENSCHWANDER

do you ever get discouraged that you can't see God? I do. God knows us better than anyone else, yet we can't see or touch him. I want to be able to see his facial expressions as I pour out my heart to him. I want to be able to be hugged by him when I need to be comforted. I want to be able to look into his eyes and see the love that he has for me! But I can't do any of these things because he isn't "there."

Yet the lyrics of this song remind me that I *have* seen God. Not directly, but through his creation. There was the time that I was walking a friend's dog and suddenly became surrounded by a warm wind with swirling leaves. God was there. In fact, I'm *sure* that he hugged me! Or the time during a worship service that the congregation was singing about God's raining his love on us . . . and as we sang, rain began to pour outside! God was acknowledging that he is always listening, and he heard our request for his love and comfort. Sunsets, flowers, children's laughter . . . the list of the ways I have seen God is infinite.

The line of this song that really sticks with me is: "And no one, nobody, is explaining you to me." During these mysterious moments, no one had to explain to me what was happening. I just knew that these beautiful moments were from God. Who else would send hope in a sunrise? or comfort in the wind? God knew that we would need to experience and understand his beauty, so he provided us with the ability to see him through our surroundings. God's creation praises him for his glory; how can we keep from doing the same?!

"Let the sea resound, and everything in it, the world, and all who live in it. Let the rivers clap their hands, let the mountains sing together for joy; let them sing before the LORD" (Psalm 98:7-9, *NIV*).

/// YOUR CUE ///

Where have you seen God?

_____
_____
_____
_____
_____
_____
_____
_____
_____

Was there a specific encounter that helped make your relationship with God more intimate?

_____
_____
_____
_____
_____
_____
_____
_____
_____
_____

Is there something in your life that is blocking you from seeing God in unexpected places? What do you need to do to change that?

_____

_____

_____

_____

_____

_____

_____

_____

_____

_____

Take time this week to see God in his creation.

_____

_____

_____

_____

TENT IN THE CENTER OF TOWN

// PERFORMED BY SARA GROVES //

There's a tent in the center of town
The people have gathered around
Cause they think they'll go there to see
lions and bears
In the tent in the center of town

But it's all about the winning of souls
Say the signs on the telephone poles
They say if you are blue Jesus is calling
you
To the tent in the center of town

The preacher is preaching his best
And he barely takes time for a breath
Their hearts are complete in the bearable
heat
In the tent in the center of town

The gentlemen all give up their seats
To the women who've been on their feet
But it's standing room only when the
Holy of Holies
Enters the center of town

There's a tent in the center of town
Where the people can gather around
Who wouldn't step foot in a church
But who aren't afraid of a good news
crusade
In the tent in the center of town

They say they're drawn in by the stripes
on the awning
And the beautiful music inside
But they're drawn by the Spirit that's
pouring down
On the tent in the center of town

And revival hits like a wave
And hundreds are joyously saved
And the thief and adulterer lay it all on
the altar
In the tent in the center of town

The time has come to move on
To the next hurting throng
And they hope as they tear it apart
The tent will live on in their hearts

I once was lost, but now I'm found
Because of a tent in the center of town

/// IT'S WORTH THE RISK ///

TABITHA NEUENSCHWANDER

ho led you to Christ? Was it a youth leader, your parents, a TV evangelist, a friend, or even a random person on the street? It really doesn't matter who led you to Christ. What matters is that someone did. Telling others about Christ can be a scary thing, and "good reasons" not to do it come all too easily when an opportunity arises. It's easy to think you don't have enough knowledge about the Bible or that you're not a good communicator. Those things may be true. But what evangelism comes down to is simply telling others about Christ's sacrifice and how it has changed your life—and no one knows that better than you. God will take it from there.

In the past I was one of those people who claimed to lack the communication skills and Bible knowledge necessary to share Christ with others. And I still claim that I am not an excellent communicator or a theologian, but I know they are not good excuses. Because Jesus commands us to share the gospel with others, I've had to get out of my comfort zone and start being more open with sharing what God has done for me. It's been scary, but each time I share, I gain more confidence. If we all kept Christ's love to ourselves, where would Christianity be?

Sara Groves does a great job of reminding us of the importance of sharing God's love. The first time I heard this song, I wanted to be in the tent in the center of town. Cheesy—I know—but the energy that flowed from hundreds being "joyously saved" was inspiring. The tent evangelists had put tons of work into drawing people into their tent and were rewarded by having people turn their lives over to Christ. The tent evangelists provided a safe environment, and people were willing to lay out their sins on the altar. It reminded me that all we have to do is put ourselves out there and God will use us—regardless of our style of evangelism.

Someone took the time to tell you. Maybe it's time to perpetuate the favor. . . .

PRAYER FOCUS

Ask God to use your weakness for his glory. Ask God to help you share his love with someone during the next month.

/// YOUR CUE ///

What weaknesses are you using as excuses not to share Christ's love with others?

_____

_____

_____

_____

_____

_____

_____

_____

_____

_____

_____

Where do you think you would be if someone hadn't shared Christ's love with you?

_____

_____

_____

_____

_____

_____

_____

_____

_____

_____

List three people with whom you need to share Christ's love.

_____

_____

_____

_____

_____

_____

_____

_____

_____